EDUCATION
Opposing Viewpoints ®

OTHER BOOKS OF RELATED INTEREST

OPPOSING VIEWPOINTS SERIES

American Values
Censorship
Child Welfare
Culture Wars
Immigration
The Information Revolution
Juvenile Crime
Teenage Pregnancy

CURRENT CONTROVERSIES SERIES

Computers and Society

AT ISSUE SERIES

Affirmative Action
Rape on Campus
Sex Education

EDUCATION

Opposing Viewpoints ®

Mary E. Williams, Book Editor

David L. Bender, Publisher
Bruno Leone, Executive Editor
Bonnie Szumski, Editorial Director
David M. Haugen, Managing Editor

OPPOSING
VIEWPOINTS®
SERIES

Greenhaven Press, Inc., San Diego, California

Cover photo: Eyewire, Inc./Corbis Corp.

Library of Congress Cataloging-in-Publication Data

Education : opposing viewpoints / Mary E. Williams, book editor.
        p.   cm. — (Opposing viewpoints series)
    Includes bibliographical references (p.   ) and index.
    ISBN 0-7377-0124-2 (pbk. : alk. paper). —
ISBN 0-7377-0125-0 (lib. bdg. : alk. paper)
    1. Public schools—United States. 2. School choice—United States.
3. Multicultural education—United States. 4. Religion in the public
schools—United States. I. Williams, Mary E., 1960–   . II. Series:
Opposing viewpoints series (Unnumbered)
LA217.2.E37 2000
371.01'0973—dc21   99-25737
                                                                          CIP

Greenhaven Press, Inc., P.O. Box 289009
San Diego, CA 92198-9009

"CONGRESS SHALL MAKE NO LAW...ABRIDGING THE FREEDOM OF SPEECH, OR OF THE PRESS."

First Amendment to the U.S. Constitution

The basic foundation of our democracy is the First Amendment guarantee of freedom of expression. The Opposing Viewpoints Series is dedicated to the concept of this basic freedom and the idea that it is more important to practice it than to enshrine it.

CONTENTS

Why Consider Opposing Viewpoints?

"The only way in which a human being can make some approach to knowing the whole of a subject is by hearing what can be said about it by persons of every variety of opinion and studying all modes in which it can be looked at by every character of mind. No wise man ever acquired his wisdom in any mode but this."

John Stuart Mill

In our media-intensive culture it is not difficult to find differing opinions. Thousands of newspapers and magazines and dozens of radio and television talk shows resound with differing points of view. The difficulty lies in deciding which opinion to agree with and which "experts" seem the most credible. The more inundated we become with differing opinions and claims, the more essential it is to hone critical reading and thinking skills to evaluate these ideas. Opposing Viewpoints books address this problem directly by presenting stimulating debates that can be used to enhance and teach these skills. The varied opinions contained in each book examine many different aspects of a single issue. While examining these conveniently edited opposing views, readers can develop critical thinking skills such as the ability to compare and contrast authors' credibility, facts, argumentation styles, use of persuasive techniques, and other stylistic tools. In short, the Opposing Viewpoints Series is an ideal way to attain the higher-level thinking and reading skills so essential in a culture of diverse and contradictory opinions.

In addition to providing a tool for critical thinking, Opposing Viewpoints books challenge readers to question their own strongly held opinions and assumptions. Most people form their opinions on the basis of upbringing, peer pressure, and personal, cultural, or professional bias. By reading carefully balanced opposing views, readers must directly confront new ideas as well as the opinions of those with whom they disagree. This is not to simplistically argue that everyone who reads opposing views will—or should—change his or her opinion. Instead, the series enhances readers' understanding of their own views by encouraging confrontation with opposing ideas. Careful examination of others' views can lead to the readers' understanding of the logical inconsistencies in their own opinions, perspective on

9

why they hold an opinion, and the consideration of the possibility that their opinion requires further evaluation.

EVALUATING OTHER OPINIONS

To ensure that this type of examination occurs, Opposing Viewpoints books present all types of opinions. Prominent spokespeople on different sides of each issue as well as well-known professionals from many disciplines challenge the reader. An additional goal of the series is to provide a forum for other, less known, or even unpopular viewpoints. The opinion of an ordinary person who has had to make the decision to cut off life support from a terminally ill relative, for example, may be just as valuable and provide just as much insight as a medical ethicist's professional opinion. The editors have two additional purposes in including these less known views. One, the editors encourage readers to respect others' opinions—even when not enhanced by professional credibility. It is only by reading or listening to and objectively evaluating others' ideas that one can determine whether they are worthy of consideration. Two, the inclusion of such viewpoints encourages the important critical thinking skill of objectively evaluating an author's credentials and bias. This evaluation will illuminate an author's reasons for taking a particular stance on an issue and will aid in readers' evaluation of the author's ideas.

As series editors of the Opposing Viewpoints Series, it is our hope that these books will give readers a deeper understanding of the issues debated and an appreciation of the complexity of even seemingly simple issues when good and honest people disagree. This awareness is particularly important in a democratic society such as ours in which people enter into public debate to determine the common good. Those with whom one disagrees should not be regarded as enemies but rather as people whose views deserve careful examination and may shed light on one's own.

Thomas Jefferson once said that "difference of opinion leads to inquiry, and inquiry to truth." Jefferson, a broadly educated man, argued that "if a nation expects to be ignorant and free . . . it expects what never was and never will be." As individuals and as a nation, it is imperative that we consider the opinions of others and examine them with skill and discernment. The Opposing Viewpoints Series is intended to help readers achieve this goal.

David L. Bender & Bruno Leone,
Series Editors

INTRODUCTION

"Intellectually and morally, America's educational system is failing far too many people."

—Signatories of "A Nation Still at Risk," 1998

In 1983, the U.S. Department of Education released a report, *A Nation at Risk*, that proclaimed that the quality of public education had deteriorated since the 1950s. The average SAT scores of college-bound seniors had fallen sixteen points, students were scoring much lower on standardized tests than their counterparts in other industrialized nations, and the dropout rate had risen. Fifteen years later, in April 1998, a group of educators, policymakers, and business leaders representing various points on the political spectrum gathered at a conference sponsored by the Heritage Foundation and several other organizations to discuss what had happened with American education since *A Nation at Risk* had been printed. Their conclusions were announced in an education reform manifesto entitled "A Nation Still at Risk," published in the July/August 1998 issue of the conservative journal *Policy Review*.

According to "A Nation Still at Risk," the quality of U.S. public education remains poor. Moreover, Americans have become complacent about educational issues because the nation's economy has been flourishing. But recent data indicate that American students are often woefully unprepared for college and for the workforce. The results of the Third International Math and Science Study, for example, show U.S. twelfth-graders placing nineteenth out of twenty-one industrialized nations in math and sixteenth out of twenty-one in science. Since 1983, more than 10 million students have reached their senior year with no basic reading skills, and 20 million have been promoted to the twelfth grade without having learned math fundamentals. During this same period, more than 6 million students dropped out of school—a number that includes from 10 to 20 percent of school-age African Americans and first-generation Hispanics. Although some educational gains have occurred since 1983—such as a rise in college attendance and an increasing willingness among high school students to take more challenging classes—academic achievement continues to lag. "The risk posed to tomorrow's well-being by the sea of educational mediocrity that still engulfs us is acute," contend the writers of the 1998 education report. "Large numbers of students remain at risk."

Parents, educators, and policymakers have responded in myriad ways to these dire reports on the state of American education. Many have pushed for reforms—such as the use of state-funded tuition vouchers and the development of charter schools—that would allow parents to choose which school their children attend. Such reforms would enable poor parents to use state funds to send their children to high-quality private schools and allow nongovernmental groups to use public money to operate their own schools. Some education scholars, however, have charged that the "education crisis" is largely a myth concocted by conservatives. According to David C. Berliner and Bruce J. Biddle, authors of *The Manufactured Crisis: Myths, Fraud, and the Attack on America's Public Schools*, conservative critics of public schools have used distorted data on student achievement with the intent of winning approval and taxpayer support for private schools. These misguided schemes for education reform could drain needed funds away from public institutions and "seriously damage American schools," contend Berliner and Biddle.

Whether or not they agree that American education has reached a crisis state, most educators believe that the public school system needs improvement. One reform measure that has received wide support among conservatives and liberals is the push for national academic standards. Currently, because public schools are administered at the state and local levels, academic standards vary widely from region to region. National standards, however, would clearly identify what concepts and skills all U.S. students should master at certain grade levels. The signatories of "A Nation Still at Risk" maintain that "America needs solid national academic standards and . . . standards-based assessments, shielded from government control, and independent of partisan politics, interest groups, and fads." These standards would give educators distinct guidelines in tracking student progress and in deciding on curricula and teaching techniques. Proponents contend that national standards would, in the end, increase academic achievement and ensure that all U.S. students receive roughly the same education.

Critics of national standards, on the other hand, fear that their implementation could lead to increased governmental intrusion in local school board decisions. Despite policymakers' assurances to the contrary, these critics argue that national standards will create politically motivated controversies over what kind of information should be taught in schools. Conservative groups such as the Christian Coalition, for example, contend that national standards could eventually impose an overly liberal

13

and secular curriculum on those who hold traditional Christian beliefs. They support local control of academic standards, arguing that local communities know best what kind of knowledge their students should learn. Conservative commentator Phyllis Schlafly agrees, adding that standards-based national testing would further undermine public education: "The new mission of the public schools would be to coach children on how to pass the test. In the end, all children will get a passing score (so as not to damage their self-esteem) and none will be permitted to excel."

Some liberals, too, oppose national standards. They often contend that such standards would prove to be frustrating for low-income school districts that cannot afford to hire better teachers, revise curricula, or renovate crumbling classrooms. Marian Wright Edelman, head of the Children's Defense Fund, maintains that it is wrong to "hold all children to the same standards without providing all children with equal [educational] resources." In fact, Edelman and others argue, setting higher academic standards for students in poor districts will damage morale and raise dropout rates when these students fail to meet these standards. Policymakers must first address the problem of educational funding inequities before setting tough national standards, these critics assert.

This broad range of concerns and suggestions for education reform reveals that there is no quick solution to the nation's educational problems. *Education: Opposing Viewpoints* examines the state of public schools and explores how education can be improved for the current and future generations of America's youth. The authors debate some of the most discussed issues in education: What Is the State of Public Education? Should Parents Be Allowed to Choose Their Children's Schools? Are Multicultural Approaches Good for Education? What Role Should Religious and Moral Values Play in Public Education? How Could Public Education Be Improved? The viewpoints presented in this volume will give readers insight into the complexity of the national debates on education and education reform.

CHAPTER 1

WHAT IS THE STATE OF PUBLIC EDUCATION?

Chapter Preface

According to a 1996 poll conducted by the *Washington Post*, 62 percent of Americans believe that the quality of the U.S. educational system has declined and that public schools "will get worse instead of better." Falling test scores, startling gaps in general knowledge among high school students, and an increasing need for remedial coursework in English and math are evidence of this educational decline, critics contend. Between the mid-1960s and the mid-1990s, for example, the average Scholastic Assessment Test (SAT) score dropped fifty-five points on the verbal section and twenty-three points on the math section. According to another standardized test conducted by the National Assessment of Educational Progress, half of all seventeen-year-olds cannot calculate the area of a rectangle, and only 20 percent are able to write a one-paragraph letter to apply for a supermarket job. Education critics blame a variety of factors—including family decline, lowered academic standards, poorly trained teachers, and school mismanagement—for this apparent deterioration of American education.

Some observers, however, argue that such claims of a public-education crisis are exaggerated. They point out that the drop in the average SAT score is not an accurate indicator of student progress because school populations have changed since the mid-1960s, when most students who took the test were wealthy and educationally privileged. "When America democratized higher education by opening up the doors of the universities to millions of middle- and working-class people, to black, brown, poor, and rural people, SAT scores dropped only 5 percent below those of the wealthy elite," argues education professor David C. Berliner. "It's a miracle how well ordinary American youth performed against the . . . privileged classes . . . [it's] a triumph for public education." Others point to the scores on the Iowa Test of Basic Skills, which have risen since the 1980s, as evidence of increasing academic achievement.

While analysts and observers generally agree that America's public school system needs improvement, some dispute the claim that the U.S. is facing an educational crisis. The authors in the following chapter present differing opinions on the state of public education and on several factors that may hinder its progress.

| "College-bound youngsters over the past two decades have not received the quality education they deserve."

THE QUALITY OF PUBLIC EDUCATION HAS DECLINED

Karl Zinsmeister

In the following viewpoint, Karl Zinsmeister argues that the caliber of American public education has declined since the mid-1960s. He reports that a drop in the average SAT score, as well as recently documented gaps in general knowledge among high school students, reveal a deterioration in the quality of education. Antitraditional school reforms, lowered standards, lightweight curricula, and undemanding coursework have created this crisis in public education, Zinsmeister contends. Zinsmeister is editor-in-chief of the *American Enterprise*, a conservative journal of opinion.

As you read, consider the following questions:

1. Between the mid-1960s and the mid-1990s, by how many points did SAT scores fall, according to Zinsmeister?
2. According to the U.S. Secretary of Education, cited by the author, what percentage of American high school seniors can read at their grade level?
3. In Zinsmeister's opinion, why have rigorous, challenging
   · classes fallen into disfavor among today's students?

Excerpted from Karl Zinsmeister, "The Sixties Rules in Public Schools," *The American Enterprise*, May/June 1997. Reprinted with permission from *The American Enterprise*, a Washington, D.C.–based magazine of politics, business, and culture.

Celebration, Florida . . . is a town being developed near Orlando by the Walt Disney Company. Because it has been carefully conceived to be a livable and practical community, with vast resources and talent being poured into it, the town promises to exert great influence over the design of future communities around the United States.

At its heart, Celebration is based on the idea that American communities prior to World War II were more livable than most modern suburbs or cities, and that new communities ought therefore be designed much more like those traditional towns. But one important community institution in Celebration is being built along lines that are anything but traditional. And that is the community school. . . .

The Celebration school will feature "the latest in educational thinking": No grades (too competitive, not "meaningful"). No set grade levels (students of various ages and skills will be mixed in "neighborhoods"). Few desks (they discourage cooperation and impose hierarchy). And so forth.

Unstructured "open school" reforms of these sorts are very trendy right now. The director of a federally funded education laboratory told a national "education summit" a few years ago that "we are no longer teaching facts to children," because "none of us can guess what information they will need in the future."

SCHOOL REFORM?

American Enterprise contributing editor Phil Langdon reports that when he recently drove by the Pennsylvania high school he attended in the early 1960s—where the principal used to write stern yearbook messages like "The north wind made the Vikings strong"—the building sported signs announcing "Teachers at Work Building Self-Esteem."

The public school my own son attended in the shadow of Cornell University in the early 1990s is organized on exactly the same principles as the Celebration school. Here, the aversion to structure, tradition, and order extends even to numerals—classrooms are no longer numbered, but referred to by names like "Moon," "Rainforest," and "Skycloud."

Contrary to their own claims, today's free-form schools are not actually built on "the latest" in educational thinking, but rather on something a full generation older. They are founded on a classic 1960s vision that children don't need to be taught so much as freed to express the wisdom that is innate within them. That such schools are springing up like mushrooms is no surprise: '60s kids are taking over as principals, teachers, and superintendents, while baby boomers-turned-yuppies provide the children for their experiments. What is surprising is that so few parents have bothered to find out whether these anti-traditional schools really work as promised.

THE UNIMPRESSIVE OUTPUT OF AMERICAN CLASSROOMS

The best-known indicator of our educational droop over the last 30 years is the average Scholastic Assessment Test (SAT) score of college-bound high school seniors. From the mid-1960s to the mid-1990s, scores fell from 478 to 423 on the verbal section, and from 502 to 479 on the math section. (On each section, everyone gets 200 points just for showing up, and a perfect score is 800.) Other test results in specific subjects like geography, reading, mathematics and calculus, biology, chemistry, and physics also show slippage—in comparison both to previous performances and to students in other industrial nations. This despite a gale of rhetoric and a huge flood of money aimed at educational improvement. From 1980 to 1996, nationwide spending per public-school student zoomed up 50 percent after inflation.

The clearest picture of contemporary miseducation comes from looking at specific knowledge gaps among today's students. Consider some of the answers given recently by 17-year-old Americans on the federal government's National Assessment of Educational Progress:

- One-third thought Columbus reached the New World after 1750.
- 62 percent were unable to place the Civil War in the years between 1850 and 1900.
- One-third had no idea what Brown v. Board of Education changed.
- A third couldn't identify the countries the U.S. fought against in World War II.
- A third couldn't identify Abraham Lincoln.
- 47 percent couldn't express the fraction $\frac{9}{100}$ as a percent.
- Half couldn't calculate the area of a rectangle. Only 6 percent are proficient in what was considered high school mathematics a generation ago (algebra, geometry, multi-step problem solving).
- A scant 6 percent could solve this problem: "Christine borrows $850 for one year from the Friendly Finance Company. If she pays 12 percent simple interest on the loan, what will be the total amount that Christine repays?"
- One-third did not know that the Mississippi River flows into the Gulf of Mexico.

- Only 20 percent could write a simple one-paragraph letter to a local supermarket manager applying for a job.

Other sources come up with similar results. Surveys done for the National Geographic Society, for instance, show that only 45 percent of 18- to 24-year-olds are able to locate New York State on a map. A third can find Michigan, a quarter Massachusetts. On a world map, just 36 percent can identify England. In 1993, Bill Clinton's Secretary of Education reported that sophisticated new reading comprehension tests show that only 37 percent of all high school seniors can read at their grade level. Fully a third of today's college students must enroll in a remedial course in reading, writing, or math when they hit campus.

© Wicks/Rothco. Reprinted with permission.

Employers, too, are distraught. Noting that 44 percent of the job-seekers who showed up at his office couldn't read at the ninth-grade level, Prudential Insurance executive Robert Winters mourned that "they are 17 years old and virtually unemployable for life." Eighty percent of the candidates for factory work at Motorola reportedly flunk the company exam seeking fifth-grade math competency and seventh-grade English levels.

And if you think this problem is limited to a few inner-city schools, think again. Today's widespread middle-class complacency on school quality is not justified. American schools are actually doing slightly better than they used to for their lowest achievers; it's at the middle and the top of the achievement scale that results have really deteriorated.

THE EROSION OF STANDARDS

Standards at American schools were higher in the past than they are today. Educator Daniel Singal compares national surveys from the 1990s and the mid-1960s ("just before countercultural innovations swept away the old curriculum") and finds that the pre-reform high school students were, for instance, more than twice as likely to write critical papers on the literary works they were studying.

At the same time the workload was declining, grades were inflating. Three decades ago, only one college-bound senior in eight carried an A average for his high school years. Today, fully one in four factors out as an A overall. (This despite the fact that a much bigger proportion of each class is in the college-bound group.)

"Every generation of students has wanted to take it easy," summarizes Virginia teacher Pat Welsh, "but until the last couple of decades, they weren't allowed to get away with it." Professor Singal agrees. "The percentage of students who are truly lazy . . . is probably no greater today than it has been in the past. The real problem, I'm convinced, is that college-bound youngsters over the past two decades have not received the quality education they deserve."

Our "dumbing-down" of the curriculum began with "the cultural ferment of the 1960s," says Singal.

> In every conceivable fashion the reigning ethos of those times was hostile to excellence in education. Individual achievement fell under intense suspicion, as did attempts to maintain standards. Discriminating among students on the basis of ability or performance was branded "elitist." Education gurus of the day called for essentially non-academic schools, whose main purpose would be to build habits of social cooperation and equality rather than to train the mind.

Because of this disdain for high achievement, says Singal, "in place of 'stretching' students, the key objective in previous eras, the goal has become not to 'stress' them.". . .

> The prevailing ideology holds that it is much better to give up the prospect of excellence than to take the chance of injuring any student's self-esteem. Instead of trying to spur children on to set high standards for themselves, teachers invest their energies in making sure that slow learners do not come to think of themselves as failures. . . .

This coddling strategy misunderstands human psychology and the means by which low achievers are best led to improved results. "Students do respond to challenge when they see it is in their best interests to do so," says Pat Welsh, a classroom veteran. But in the aftermath of the '60s we are afraid to ask for hard work and high achievement.

SUPERFICIAL LEARNING

Some time ago, I opened my local paper and read an article describing how teenagers at a school just down the street spent several weeks of afternoon classes making "Medusa masks." A local "performance artist and storyteller" first read them the Greek Medusa myth, then students sketched and eventually modelled plaster likenesses. The teacher leading the class said she chose to have the teenagers (who were not art students) make a mask because "it wipes away your identity so you can become something you would never have allowed otherwise."

Students picked up on this. One reported "I felt like with the different masks . . . I could be anything I want to be. I could say more. I could say anything I want to." Another student said the project was fun. "I wish the whole day was art, art, art," exclaimed 14-year-old Ramadan Muhammad, who expressed hopes of becoming a doctor.

The large photo accompanying the article is, to be honest, somewhat embarrassing to look at. Here is a circle of strapping young men and women surrounded by styrofoam egg cartons, baby food jars full of bright paint, and crude papier-mâché Halloween masks—looking worrisomely like preschoolers at "crafts time."

Superficial learning of this sort is now endemic in U.S. schools, at all age levels. Friends whose children attend Seattle public schools shared a letter they sent to the principal of their fourth-grader's school:

> In mathematics . . . the "Homework Times" for the week takes less than an hour of work and includes no drilling or substantial sets of problems to be solved. . . . Matthew's science work for the last two weeks has included work on insects, including at least four class periods spent on drawing an imaginary insect and sharing it with the class. This seems creative, but not rigorous. As far as we can determine Matthew has not been required to read any book in the last two weeks, nor to report on one. . . . He has apparently not had a social studies class in two weeks . . . last week's frivolous "Homework Times" assignment required Matthew (among other things) to find out the birthdays of three popular entertainers.

LIGHTWEIGHT CURRICULA

Nice middle-class schools all across this country are now cursed with lightweight curricula and undemanding instruction of this sort. Because these institutions don't have high dropout rates and outright illiteracy, parents think these schools are not part of today's educational problem. They're wrong. Low standards plague even our very best schools.

In an article in the *Wall Street Journal*, parent and college-level educator Barbara Bronson Gray reflects on her children's experience in their suburban California school, which was nominated for the U.S. Education Department's Blue Ribbon School Award.

> The work the children bring home [is] often not corrected, with spelling and grammar errors un-noted. . . . Some of the teachers say that correcting children's written work inhibits the writing process and lowers their self-esteem. . . . Remember book reports? You not only had to remember what you read, but learn to summarize and analyze and get it down on paper. Not any more. At this school, the kids make mobiles and dioramas to illustrate the book's concept. As for writing, most of what is taught is creative writing, journal writing, free expression. Learn the structure of a paragraph? How to research a topic? How to argue a point? No, that's old-fashioned. Boring.

What's sad, comments Gray, is that these kids are well-prepared for academic challenge. The school is located in a neighborhood where "the average family's income approaches $70,000 and most of the parents have college degrees. This is a place where Cub Scouts and Brownies and soccer and baseball and karate and all kinds of after-school activities are widely available." Prepared or not, though, challenge is not what the local kids are getting at school. . . .

MAKING SCHOOL "RELEVANT" AND "FUN"

American students have been encouraged by their baby-boomer teachers to believe that education has to be fun. Consequently, the resistance to any learning that might seem dry or strenuous has become quite strong. Moviemaker George Lucas, of *Indiana Jones* and *Star Wars* fame, is one of scores of vendors now capitalizing on this by selling television-based "education" packages to school districts. Another "no-sweat education" craze today is "Internet learning." The benefits are quite limited. The expenses are very high. But there is lots of novelty value and little student or teacher pain, so resources are pouring in.

Structurally, many public high school administrators have remade their institutions into what has been called "the shopping mall school," where teenagers pick and choose their education à la carte. With no requirements and few encouragements for students to tackle rigorous material, difficult classes have fallen into disfavor. A few years ago, reporters from the *Los Angeles Times* paid a visit to suburban Northridge Middle School. They found classes in "baseball-card collecting, jigsaw puzzles, and crocheting." A Northridge teacher volunteered that "the most important job in junior high is not subject matter, but morale."

The late sociologist James Coleman, who studied this phenomenon, noted that when the '60s demand for "relevant" courses seeped down to the high school level, the result was that "foreign languages shrank to a shadow of the curriculum, while college-preparatory mathematics, physics, and chemistry went into a less steep decline. These unpopular subjects were replaced by film-making, mystery novels, and other courses that had the appeal of little homework . . . minimal demands on analytical skills, and some connection to popular culture."

Education expert Chester Finn reports that what students know best today comes from popular culture. They are, in particular, familiar with historical figures and literary characters who have been translated into movies and television shows. "What they know least are the books, ideas, events, and authors taught only in school."

The problem with encouraging students to expect that they'll be amused at school, cautions professor Harry Wray, is that education "isn't always fun. . . . It only becomes fun after we have had to memorize something. . . . Interest develops from that base." (Wray, who teaches in Japan, suggests that "Japanese students are more realistic about school." They "have been socialized to assume that they are in school to learn. They do not expect to be entertained.") . . .

The Need to Clarify Goals

It's highly desirable that American schools should encourage creativity, and be flexible in the ways they operate. And there is nothing wrong with educational experimentation, so long as it is disciplined, hard-nosed, and carefully monitored to make sure it produces results. Nor is there anything wrong with today's children—who are as talented and knowledge-hungry as any previous.

Our problem is that many of today's teachers and parents absorbed the anti-authority, anti-excellence ideology of the '60s, and as a result often fail to inspire or direct the young authoritatively. "Instead of offering challenges and clearly defined goals, we prefer to let kids slide by, for fear that many won't choose to work toward those goals," says Pat Welsh, the teacher.

This approach claims to be compassionate, but in fact it robs all children, and especially the least advantaged, of the chance to excel. Only high standards, clear direction, and genuine achievement in the face of stiff demands will ever stretch children to their full human potential. Saint Augustine put his finger on it long ago: We must raise our goals if we are to meet them.

> "America's schools miraculously have maintained or improved achievement during the last 25 years."

THE QUALITY OF PUBLIC EDUCATION HAS NOT DECLINED

David C. Berliner

David C. Berliner is a professor of education at Arizona State University in Tempe and coauthor of *The Manufactured Crisis: Myth, Fraud, and the Attack on America's Public Schools*. In the following viewpoint, Berliner maintains that the quality of public education has not deteriorated over the past few decades. The drop in SAT scores is actually small, considering that today's students—including many underprivileged minorities and working-class people—are being compared to wealthy, Ivy League–bound students who took the SAT in 1941. Moreover, the author asserts, other standardized tests reveal gains in reading, writing, math, and science. Berliner grants that schools serving disadvantaged students in poor districts often lack educational quality; on the whole, however, U.S. public education has enhanced academic achievement since the 1970s.

As you read, consider the following questions:

1. According to Berliner, what is the purpose of the SAT?
2. How did the advent of television affect SAT scores, in the author's opinion?
3. What social factors have made it increasingly difficult for parents to raise high-achieving children, in Berliner's view?

I t seems that every generation condemns the schools its children attend. Many of today's school critics are nostalgic for a past that certainly was not nearly as nice as they remember it. In 1959, an "education crisis" was declared by Adm. Hyman Rickover, who insisted that America's schools were failures, and that unless things changed radically, it was inevitable that the United States would lose in economic and military competition with the better-educated Russians. *Reader's Digest* and other popular magazines of the fifties reported that students could not identify major cities in the United States, write literate essays or solve simple math problems. America was said to be pursuing affective goals, not paying attention to basic academics, failing to set common educational standards and, even worse, ignoring religion in the schools.

If these criticisms from 40 to 50 years ago sound familiar, it's because the same ones are trotted out every few years by an older generation unhappy with its youth. After all, criticism of our public schools is as American as apple pie and has been going on since they were founded. Playwright Jane Wagner had it right when she observed that humans developed language because of their deep inner need to complain! Today, however, complaints about the public schools are so widespread that most Americans are beginning to believe the schools actually have failed. That is not so. Let us look at the facts.

THE SCHOLASTIC ASSESSMENT TEST

Although the decline in average scores on the Scholastic Assessment Tests, or SAT, is real, it actually represents a triumph for American education. Former Education Secretary William Bennett and other conservatives repeatedly cite the decline in SAT scores as "proof" that students are dumber, teachers don't deliver, business is doomed to failure and our nation is at risk. But Bennett, who now edits books on virtue, has not been completely honest with the American people. He has neglected to mention that the SAT is an aptitude test, which predicts the future (in this case, college grades). The SAT does not assess the past; that is what an achievement test does.

Bennett has used the SAT as if it measured school achievement on a representative sample of high-school students, but it isn't designed for that. The SAT simply predicts the likelihood of success during the first year of college. There are no scales assessing social studies, history, art or music, and none on science. The test does not measure what kids have studied in school. By calling the test an achievement test Bennett violates the guidelines issued by the the test developers and all the experts in assessment. But uninformed critics continue to interpret the test in an invalid way.

The conservative critics also say the average scores dropped 90 points between the early sixties and the mid-seventies, and that certainly scared a lot of Americans. However, those were not raw points but "scaled" points. Think of it this way: When a hockey team gets four goals, it gets a score of 4; when a football team makes four goals, it may get a score of 28, but it only scored four times. So the SAT didn't really go down 90 points, it dropped about seven raw score items, a loss of 5 percent over more than 30 years. That's not nearly as scary as a 90-point drop, and it seems unlikely that America has been ruined because of this small drop in correct answers to multiple-choice test items.

In fact, the drop is remarkably small, considering the fact that the graduating high-school students of 50 years ago, whose scores set a benchmark for the scores of today's students, were not ordinary people. They predominantly were from wealthy families living in the Northeast. Almost half of them had attended private schools, and most of them wanted to go to the Ivy schools such as Yale and Harvard. This elite group took the first SATs in 1941, a year when fewer than 40 percent of ordinary American youth graduated high school. When America democratized higher education by opening up the doors of the universities to millions of middle- and working-class people, to black, brown, poor and rural people, SAT test scores dropped only 5 percent below those of the wealthy elite. It's a miracle how well ordinary American youth performed against the 1941 privileged classes. It's something for which Americans should be proud, a triumph for public education.

The change in the types of people who took the SAT accounted for most of the decline in scores that began in 1963. But the drop was predominantly in the verbal part of the test, which reflects the advent of television. The average young person raised after 1950 watched about 20,000 hours of TV before high-school graduation. In 1963 the first students raised with television began graduating from our high schools. Increased TV watching resulted in less reading and, consequently, some decline in verbal test scores.

GAINS IN ACADEMIC ACHIEVEMENT

America does, however, have valid tests to measure school achievement, notably the National Assessment of Educational

Progress, or NAEP. From the 1970s to the mid-1990s average NAEP-test scores are rock steady or show gains in reading, writing, science and math.

More importantly, however, the test scores remained steady or rose while the quality of life for American youth was going down. Currently, one in four young people lives below the official poverty level—the highest rate for all industrialized democracies. Increasingly, American mothers lack adequate prenatal care, so more American babies suffer from low birth weight. These same children receive less postnatal medical care than is available in other industrialized democracies. Increasingly, youth in this country live in single-parent households or families in which both parents work, making it more difficult to raise high-achieving children. Increasingly, American youth suffer the effects of violence and drugs in their neighborhoods. More youngsters than ever before have their values distorted by a media that promotes consumerism and sexuality. In spite of these deteriorating social conditions for youth, America's schools miraculously have maintained or improved achievement during the last 25 years. America should be proud of its teachers and public schools and ashamed of the inhospitable conditions created for raising children.

IMPROVED EDUCATIONAL ACHIEVEMENT

As Will Rogers put it, "The schools are not as good as they used to be and never were." But while the history of American education records no golden age, it reveals an astonishing accomplishment with the people whom the inscription on the Statue of Liberty calls the world's poor, huddled masses. Despite waves of immigrants and the inclusion of the minority poor, the level of educational attainment in the United States has steadily increased. Not only have secondary and higher education expanded enormously in the twentieth century, but, save for a decade between 1965 and 1975, the expansion has been accompanied by improved outcomes. We can continue to build on that achievement without false alarms about the Russians or the Japanese burying us in international competition.

Gerald W. Bracey, *American Prospect*, March-April 1998.

Scores on all major commercial standardized tests of achievement have risen in recent years. Tests such as the respected Iowa Test of Basic Skills, or ITBS, showed all-time high scores in the 1980s, and American youngsters busted through to even higher scores in the 1990s. Apparently America has been on a rising tide of school achievement. And no wonder—in the spring of 1996 the nation graduated from high school the largest number of students ever that had taken advanced placement (college credit) courses, the highest number ever to have a full academic schedule while in high school and the highest percent ever that planned to enter college. Not too shabby for a system reputed to be in disarray.

There is good news as well about average test scores for entrance to graduate school—either the general Graduate Record Exam or the specialized tests for law and business. Democratization of graduate education in the United States since the 1960s has meant that the number of college graduates taking these tests has risen by hundreds of percentage points. Nevertheless, the scores on all these tests went up. To open up educational opportunities in graduate school to millions of citizens with no loss of academic quality is another miracle. Apparently, the young people leaving college are smarter than the people who come to campus to interview them for jobs. Even IQ-test scores are up—with today's youth scoring about 34 percentile ranks above their grandparents and about 20 percentile ranks above their parents. Today's youth apparently are more intelligent than the adults in their families.

COMPARISONS WITH OTHER NATIONS

Finally, in the international assessments of educational achievement (financed in part by the U.S. government), America is not nearly as bad off as the school critics would have you believe, though it is not likely that the nation will win Olympic gold for its academic performance. One of the problems is that Americans have decided not to work their children in school as hard as do parents in other nations, including a decision to have many less days of formal schooling (180) per year than either Japan (240) or South Korea (225). Furthermore, the United States has a higher rate of youth employment than many countries, including Germany and Japan. And often forgotten is that American youth start dating earlier and with much greater intensity than is true in most other nations. Less time in school, more time at work and incredible amounts of time allocated to dating preclude America's youth from winning the gold.

Nevertheless, in an international reading comparison conducted by the International Evaluation of Educational Achievement in 1992, America's 9-year-olds placed second, while America's 14-year-olds tied for second. The United States placed behind little Finland, a homogeneous nation with government supports for its families and little variation in wealth and poverty. While the United States did not perform as well in math and science, some states (Minnesota, North Dakota and Iowa) matched the top performing nations (Taiwan and South Korea). Nationwide, students from advantaged homes, white students and Asian-Americans all performed at world-class levels. Interestingly, Asian-American students outperform Asian students in Asia, suggesting that American schools work well for some of their students. Not surprisingly, the poorest states (Alabama, Mississippi, Louisiana) and the poorest American students (Hispanics, the urban disadvantaged and African-Americans) performed poorly.

TWO SETS OF PUBLIC SCHOOLS

These findings demonstrate that America has two sets of public schools. One set provides world-class education for the advantaged, for majority children, for Asians and the students in our homogenous, well-supported, populist, Midwestern states. America's other public-school system operates in poor Southern states, in rural areas and in the neighborhoods of the urban poor in which most of the ethnic and racial minorities reside. America's public schools as a whole have not failed to deliver, but they have failed to deliver to certain families and certain communities.

There is indeed a crisis of achievement in some of our schools. But the conservative critics of the nation's public schools wrongly have pointed the finger at America's educators. The nation's school problems are rooted in the culture of America. And there is no little irony in the fact that the cultural problems are worsened by the very economic and social policies espoused by Bennett and his vocal friends on the extreme right.

| "The sorry state of student achievement in America is due more to the conditions of students' lives outside of school than to what takes place within school walls."

POOR COMMITMENT TO ACADEMIC ACHIEVEMENT HAMPERS PUBLIC EDUCATION

Laurence Steinberg

Laurence Steinberg is a psychology professor at Temple University in Philadelphia, Pennsylvania, and coauthor of *Beyond the Classroom: Why School Reform Has Failed and What Parents Need to Do*. In the following viewpoint, he argues that the crisis in public education is largely due to outside social factors, not specific educational standards and policies. Parental irresponsibility, after-school jobs and social activities, and a decreased commitment to academic achievement among students leaves many college-bound youth unprepared for higher education, Steinberg contends. He concludes that students and families must genuinely commit themselves to the process of education for public schools to succeed.

As you read, consider the following questions:

1. According to a recent study of the California State University system, what percentage of freshmen need remedial instruction in math?
2. How many hours per week do students spend in activities likely to contribute to learning, according to Steinberg?
3. In the author's opinion, why does after-school employment do more harm than good?

President Bill Clinton's proposal in June 1996 to widen access to postsecondary education by granting tax credits to help finance the first two years of college may be good politics in an election year. But if we don't do something to improve the quality of the students who will be entering our nation's colleges and universities, the plan will be disastrous policy. The last thing this country needs is a rising tide of mediocre students riding the educational people-mover for 14 rather than 12 years.

What we need instead is an open and candid discussion of why our high school graduates are entering college so ill-prepared for higher education.

An Unmitigated Failure

By any credible measure, the past two decades of tinkering with America's schools have been an unmitigated failure. Although there are occasional success stories about a school here or a district there that has turned students' performance around, the competence of American students overall has not improved in 25 years. The proportions of high school juniors scoring in the top categories on the math, science, reading and writing portions of national achievement tests have not changed in any meaningful way in two decades. Scholastic Assessment Test (SAT) scores have not risen since the early 1980s, and they even dropped somewhat in recent years; today they remain lower than they were in the early 1970s. A recent study of the California State University system indicated that half of all freshmen needed remedial education in math, and nearly half needed remedial education in English.

My colleagues and I recently released the results of the most extensive study ever conducted on the forces that affect youngsters' interest and performance in school. Over two years of planning and pilot-testing, four years of data collection in the field, and four years of data analysis, we studied more than 20,000 teenagers and their families in nine very different American communities. Our findings suggest that the sorry state of student achievement in America is due more to the conditions of students' lives outside of school than to what takes place within school walls. The failure of our educational policies is due to our obsession with reforming schools and classrooms, and our general disregard of the contributing forces that, while outside the boundaries of the school, are probably more influential.

According to our research, nearly one in three parents in America is seriously disengaged from his or her adolescent's life, and, especially, from the adolescent's education. Only about one-fifth of parents consistently attend school programs. Nearly one-third of students say their parents have no idea how they are doing in school. About one-sixth of all students report that their parents don't care whether they earn good grades in school.

Nor is there support for achievement within adolescent peer groups. To be sure, teen society in America has never been a strong admirer of academic accomplishment. But widespread parental disengagement has left a large proportion of adolescents far more susceptible to the influence of their friends than in past generations, and this influence is taking its toll on school achievement. Fewer than one in five students say their friends think it is important to get good grades in school. Less than one-fourth of all students regularly discuss their schoolwork with their friends. Nearly one-fifth of all students say they do not try as hard as they can in school because they are worried about what their friends might think.

It's not surprising, then, that very little of the typical American student's time—something on the order of 15 to 20 hours weekly, or only about 15% of his or her waking hours—is spent on endeavors likely to contribute to learning or achievement. In terms of how much time is expected of them for school and school-related pursuits, American students are among the least challenged in the industrialized world. Many spend more time flipping hamburgers and roaming malls than they do in school. For too many students, part-time work and after-school socializing have supplanted school-sponsored extracurricular activities—activities that help to strengthen youngsters' attachment to the school as an institution.

WHAT SHOULD BE DONE

President Clinton has called for boosting American student achievement by 2000. But before we rush once again to reinvent the curriculum, retrain our teachers, refurbish our schools' laboratories or expand access to higher education, here are several steps that must be taken:

• Change the focus of the national debate over our achievement problem from reforming schools to changing students' and parents' attitudes and behaviors. No amount of school reform will work unless we recognize the solution as considerably more far-reaching and complicated than simply changing curricular standards, teaching methods or instructional materials.

• Conduct a serious discussion about the high rate of parental irresponsibility. The widespread disengagement of parents from the business of child-rearing is a public health problem that

Mark Cullum. Reprinted by permission of Copley News Service.

warrants urgent national attention.

• Recognize that the prevailing and pervasive peer norm of "getting by" is in part a direct consequence of an educational system that neither rewards excellence nor punishes failure. The vast majority of students know all too well that the grades they earn in school will, under the present system, have little or no impact on their future educational or occupational success.

Although schools have played a role in creating this situation, they have been abetted by parents, employers and institutions of higher education. In our study, more than half of all students said they could bring home grades of "C" or worse without their parents getting upset, and one-quarter said they could bring home grades of "D" or worse without consequence. Few employers ask to see students' high school or college transcripts. With the exception of our country's most selective colleges and universities, our postsecondary educational institutions are willing to accept virtually any applicant with a high school diploma, regardless of his or her scholastic record. The current practice of providing remedial education in such basic academic skills as reading, writing and mathematics to entering college students has trivialized the significance of the high school diploma, and drained precious resources away from bona fide college-level instruction.

• Reconsider the proposition that after-school employment is inherently beneficial for teenagers. There is very little evidence that widely available after-school jobs teach students the skills

35

and competencies they will need to be successful, highly educated workers. There is considerable proof, however, that extensive after-school employment has more costs—diminished commitment to school, for instance, and increased drug and alcohol use—than benefits.

• Support school-sponsored extracurricular programs and extend them to as many students as possible. Participation in school-based extracurricular activities strengthens youngsters' commitment to school and carries benefits that spill over into the classroom, especially for students who are having difficulty in school.

• Re-establish in the minds of young people and parents that the primary activity of childhood and adolescence is schooling. If we want our children to value education and strive for achievement, adults must behave as if doing well in school—not just graduating, but actually doing well—is more important than socializing, organized sports, after-school jobs or any other activity.

FAMILIES MATTER MOST

For far too long, our national debate about education has been dominated by disputes over how schools ought to be changed without examining the other forces that affect students' willingness to learn and their ability to achieve. It is time to leave behind the myopic view that schools determine student achievement, and, most importantly, that school reform is the solution to America's achievement problem.

No curriculum overhaul, no instructional innovation, no change in school organization, no toughening of standards, no rethinking of teacher training or compensation will succeed if students do not come to school interested in, and committed to, learning. Any policy that merely increases the years of schooling, without ensuring that students and their families are committed to the education process, will be far more costly than any tax credit imaginable.

> "For the last few decades too many of our public schools have not expected the very best from our nation's youth."

LOW EXPECTATIONS HAMPER PUBLIC EDUCATION

James White

In the following viewpoint, James White contends that the low quality of today's public schools is the result of educators' low expectations. Because teachers fail to set high standards and do not expect high-quality student work, students do not achieve academic excellence. Moreover, White maintains, blaming parents or outside social factors for low student performance simply fosters laziness and mediocrity. Public schools must raise their educational standards if students are to excel, he concludes. White is a teacher in Houston, Texas, and a contributing editor for *Headway*, a monthly conservative journal.

As you read, consider the following questions:

1. According to White, why do some education experts disapprove of homework?
2. How much did per-pupil expenditures increase nationally during the 1980s, according to the author?
3. Why do students often excel in sports and extracurricular courses, in White's opinion?

Reprinted from James White, "Public Schools Crumble Under Weight of Low Expectations," *Headway*, June 1996, by permission of *Headway*.

Self-proclaimed education experts blame low student performance on everything except themselves. They often cite the lack of funds and parental involvement, or social factors, for the decline in American public education.

Alternatives for Homework?

I teach at a public middle school that is predominantly black in inner-city Houston, Texas. Recently, I suggested to our school's dean of instruction that we require our seventh grade students to turn in all homework typed. Even though many of our students do not have typewriters or computers at home, we could make the school's computers more accessible.

Reluctantly, she agreed. Then she remarked, "You know, many experts do not believe in this." Confused, I responded, "Students using technology?" "No," she replied, "homework."

Apparently, many education "experts" believe homework has more negative than positive effects. For example, these experts contend that homework distracts from quality family time. Also, as my dean of instruction stated, often the parents—not the children—do the homework. Additionally, the dean of instruction blamed low report card grades at our school on homework. Therefore, we either had to find an "alternative," or stop assigning homework.

My school's students' annual scores are well below the state averages in reading and arithmetic. Only half the students read at their grade level and just 30 percent of our students can compute at their grade level. With this type of performance on basic skills, how can anyone—parent or educator—suggest eliminating or finding an alternative for homework?

A Lack of Standards

This situation embodies the real problem in many of our public schools. They lack high standards or student expectations. Jack Christie, president of the State Board of Education in Texas, hit it dead on when he said, "It's not everywhere (poor academic performance), but it is out there." He continued, "I've substituted in classes, and helped in classes in the toughest schools, and I don't think they're demanded to perform [at a higher level]. I don't think the community, the teachers, the parents, the businesses or the principals, are getting to the children to tell them how serious it is."

It is not necessarily the lack of parental involvement, social factors, or the lack of money that account for the functional illiterates that our public schools are graduating. It is the lack of standards in too many cases that explains low student performance.

The experts will contend that the taxpaying public lacks the commitment to make all our public schools first-rate institutions. But this merely translates into the taxpayers not wanting to throw more good money after bad money. In real terms, per pupil expenditures nationally increased 29 percent during the 1980's. This was preceded by real-term increases of 27 percent and 58 percent in the '70s and '60s respectively. So, it is not taxpayers' commitment that has been lacking, but the education establishment's commitment to standards.

THE ROOT CAUSE OF LOW PERFORMANCE

Throughout the nation, teachers overwhelmingly identify parental involvement as the most important improvement that could be made in education. For the most part, they are correct. Decades of research shows a high correlation between parental satisfaction and student achievement. But eventually what matters is what happens between the students and the instructor. If the instructor does not establish and set high standards, ultimately that student's performance will be below average.

Also, educators blame social factors for poor student performance. In the most low income, crime-ridden neighborhoods, Catholic and other private schools have produced better academic results than public schools.

WHY EDUCATORS FAIL

The goal of the schools now is to inculcate self-esteem in schoolchildren instead of to give them the skills necessary for individual achievement. The schools have been pumping up kids with inflated notions of their self-worth and importance, eliminating the discipline of competition, insulating them from failure, and shielding them from the knowledge that poor performance can be remedied by hard work and perseverance.

Phyllis Schlafly Report, October 1996.

Recently, a math teacher and I discussed student math performance. I told him that during my grade school years, I remember having to complete 35–40 math problems daily for homework. He countered that expectation was unrealistic in this day and time. Students simply will not go home and complete the homework.

This is a prime example of how low student expectations are the root cause of low student performance. Only 30 percent of his students can successfully do math at their grade level, and he has capitulated on a very needed practice regimen.

HIGH EXPECTATIONS CREATE SUCCESS

During my brief career in education, I have learned that students can excel at whatever they desire. Every day on my way home, I notice black youth mastering basketball skills. Surely, if these youth committed time to reading and math, they could exhibit mastery in these subjects.

Classroom teachers often marvel at the results coaches and other extracurricular teachers get from the same students that chronically perform below average in the classroom. The identical student who could not reason mathematically, logically reasoned difficult football plays under physical and mental stress. The same student who could not read in English class, later that same day is reciting poetry by heart in drama class. Extracurricular instructors get the most out of students because they expect nothing less. Just trying is not good enough. Losing is not an option. Therefore, it is these instructors who earn the admiration and respect of the students.

Looking back at my past educational experiences, the teachers who required the most from me are the instructors that I fondly remember, respect, and ultimately thank.

When a teacher uses excuses such as social factors or changing times, he or she is fostering irresponsibility and complacency. How can an instructor ever expect a student to raise himself out of his or her deficient living standards if the teacher uses that very excuse to legitimize low expectations? This only encourages the student to adopt the victimization mentality; that is, it is "the man" or the cards that life "unfairly" dealt me as the reasons I cannot excel and become a productive citizen.

What one expects is what one gets. Expect and stress excellence, and that will be the result. But if one expects complacency and laziness, he'll get that. Unfortunately, for the last few decades too many of our public schools have not expected the very best from our nation's youth. Consequently, we have not gotten the best academic performance.

| "Our educational system is so riddled with inequities that our schools and colleges actually exacerbate the effects of race and poverty."

RACIAL AND FINANCIAL INEQUITIES HAMPER PUBLIC EDUCATION

Kati Haycock

Low-income and minority students typically receive the poorest education, argues Kati Haycock in the following viewpoint. Schools attended by minorities and the poor often have unchallenging curricula, underqualified faculty, few instructional resources, and insufficient funding, she reports. Haycock grants that public schools should make high academic standards a priority. However, she contends, poor and minority youth must also receive their fair share of educational resources if public schools intend to benefit all students. Haycock is the director of the Education Trust, a research organization. She is also vice-chair of the Poverty and Race Research Action Council in Washington, D.C.

As you read, consider the following questions:

1. According to Haycock, what percentage of science teachers in predominantly minority schools are certified in their field?
2. What percentage of African-American fourth-graders are proficient in reading, according to research cited by the author?
3. Of every one hundred Latinos, how many receive bachelor's degrees, according to Haycock?

Reprinted from Kati Haycock, "The Growing Education Gap," *Poverty & Race*, March/April 1997, by permission of *Poverty & Race*, 1711 Connecticut Ave. NW, Suite 207, Washington, DC 20009; (202) 387-9887.

Two decades of progress in narrowing the achievement gap has ended. Our report, *Education Watch: The 1996 Education Trust State and National Data Book*, finds that the gap separating low-income and minority students from other young Americans is growing once again. The study, which ranks the 50 states and the District of Columbia on 17 indicators of educational quality and equity, paints a disturbing portrait of student achievement—kindergarten through college. The report argues that the current effort to set uniformly high standards for all students, though critical, is by no means enough to close the gap once and for all.

MULTIPLE INEQUITIES

The data presented in our report suggest that our educational system is so riddled with inequities that our schools and colleges actually exacerbate the effects of race and poverty, rather than ameliorate them. Students from low-income families and students of color are far more likely to attend schools with only minimal expectations for student performance, so they have much to gain from the new movement toward high standards for all. But schools attended by low-income students and students of color are also more likely than schools attended by other young Americans to have only meager cash resources, under-prepared teachers and the most watered down curriculum. Thus, an education improvement effort that simply rolls out high standards, without attention to other inequities, will leave most students of color and low-income students behind.

In 1990, schools with low poverty levels spent an average of $6565 per student, while those with higher poverty levels spent an average of $5173 per student. However, the way school dollars are spent is as important as the amount of funds allocated. Investing resources like well-educated teachers, up-to-date textbooks and challenging curricula is especially important.

Poor children and minority children do not get their fair share of such resources. For example, while 86% of science teachers in predominantly White schools are certified in their field, only 54% of science teachers in predominantly minority schools are so certified. In low-poverty schools, fewer than 1 in 5 English classes are taught by a teacher who does not even have a minor in English, while in high-poverty schools, approximately 1 in 3 courses is so taught. And the teachers in schools serving concentrations of poor and minority children were more than twice as likely to lack books and other instructional resources as teachers in low-poverty schools.

Lower Standards for Minority Students

Our report also points out significant differences in what is taught to different groups of students. For example, students from poor families are much less likely to be placed in rigorous college preparatory classes and much more likely to be placed in watered down "general" or "vocational" courses. Similarly, African American and Latino students are less likely to be placed in courses that build high-level thinking skills, including Geometry, Algebra II and Chemistry. Even when the courses are named the same, the standards are lower. Indeed, students in high-poverty schools routinely receive "A's" for work that would receive a "C" in more affluent schools.

Minority youngsters learn less at every level. For example, among 4th graders, approximately 4 in every 10 White students are "proficient" in reading. However, only 1 in 11 African American 4th graders and 1 in 8 Latino 4th graders are proficient readers. In grade 8, approximately 1 in 3 White students is proficient in mathematics, compared to 1 in 33 African Americans and 1 in 14 Latinos.

These inequities contribute to significant differences in the educational success of different students. On the whole, African American and Latino students experience the least success. They graduate from high school, enter college and graduate from college at rates below other students. While about 25 of every 100 White young Americans obtain at least a Bachelor's Degree, among African Americans only 12 do so, and among Latinos, only 10 do so.

Achievement Gaps

In the seventies and early eighties, there was considerable progress in narrowing the achievement gap between minority students and other students. Over the course of two decades, the gap between African Americans and Whites declined by about half, and the gap between Latinos and Whites declined by about one-third.

Between 1988 and 1990, though, that progress stopped. Since then, depending on grade level and subject, it has either remained the same or grown. For example, in 1973, African Americans scored 40 points below Whites on the 12th grade NAEP (National Assessment of Educational Progress) mathematics exam. By 1990, that gap had narrowed to 21 points. Four years later, though, the gap had grown again to 27 points. Among 13-year-olds, the gap between Latinos and Whites on the NAEP math exam stood at 35 points in 1973, 19 in 1986, and 25 in 1994. The trends were similar in reading.

Success Is Possible

Clearly, none of this is inevitable. Our report profiles several successful schools, school districts and colleges. Among them are Waitz Elementary School in Mission, TX, where more than 95% of the impoverished student body passes Texas' challenging Texas Assessment of Academic Skills test—a pass rate envied by affluent schools. We also cite recent gains in New York City in the number of 9th graders passing tough Regents' Math and Science Courses and the number of well-prepared students entering the City University of New York.

While in most states African American children are severely under-represented in Advanced Placement (AP) math and science or Gifted and Talented courses, and over-represented in Special Education and suspensions, some states do better here, too. For example, African American youngsters in Ohio participate in AP and Gifted courses at slightly higher rates than do White students, and they are placed in Special Ed at about the same rate. Similarly, Latino youngsters in New York are placed in Gifted and Special Education programs at rates not appreciably different from those of other students.

"Apartheid Education"

In American public education, the status quo is a system that explicitly favors the offspring of the wealthy over poor and minority children. Because local governments provide almost half of the cost of K-12 education, differences in wealth among communities translate into disparate levels of resources for schools. Some affluent suburban school districts spend two or three times more on the education of their children than either urban or rural communities can afford.

In the case of the urban/suburban comparison, these differences also break down along racial lines, with public policy consequently favoring the education of white children over minorities. Critic Jonathan Kozol has called the system "apartheid education."

John Allen, *National Catholic Reporter*, May 2, 1997.

Around the country, there are schools and colleges that are proving every day that poor and minority students absolutely can achieve at the same high levels as other students if they are taught to high levels. Our report urges states and communities to take the important steps to increase the performance of all students:

- set high educational standards,
- assure that all students get a challenging curriculum,
- make sure all children have expert teachers.

| "Large numbers of public-school teachers are not qualified to teach the subjects to which they are assigned."

POORLY TRAINED TEACHERS HAMPER PUBLIC EDUCATION

Lawrence W. Reed

In the following viewpoint, Lawrence W. Reed argues that the low quality of teacher training hampers public education. Standards have been lowered in many liberal arts and education courses in American universities, resulting in incompetent and unqualified teachers, the author reports. Reed is president of the Mackinac Center for Public Policy, a free-market research and educational organization headquartered in Midland, Michigan.

As you read, consider the following questions:

1. According to Reed, what percentage of high-school seniors rated as proficient in science and writing in Michigan in 1996?
2. What tends to get emphasized in college freshman composition courses, according to the author?
3. In the opinion of Peter T. Koper, quoted by Reed, why is the teaching of grammar "quintessentially democratizing?"

Reprinted from Lawrence W. Reed, "The Problem of Education Doesn't End at the Twelfth Grade," *The Freeman*, January 1997, by permission of *The Freeman*.

The sad story of poor student performance in America's public schools is so widely known these days that most people greet each new study that confirms it with a kind of numbed disgust.

That was the case in my state of Michigan in September 1996 when the results of proficiency tests in math, reading, writing, and science were reported in the press. Barely one-third of high school seniors were rated proficient in science and writing and fewer than half achieved that basic level in math and reading. "So what else is new?" seemed to be the common response.

POORLY PREPARED TEACHERS

The decline in students' test scores and of literacy in America are often laid at the doorstep of K-12 public education. Children are clearly being shortchanged, but not by the K-12 system alone. Indirectly but decisively, children are being shortchanged by the system that teaches the teachers who teach the children—*higher education.*

In September 1996, the National Commission on Teaching & America's Future released an important study. The bottom line: Large numbers of public-school teachers are not qualified to teach the subjects to which they are assigned. Close inspection suggests that the problem is not that too few teachers are graduating with good grades and degrees in education; the problem is what goes on in the courses they take from university departments of education.

Poor student performance and poor teacher preparation are directly related. In a recent study for the Mackinac Center for Public Policy, Professor Thomas Bertonneau argued that general undergraduate instruction in the state universities is deficient and deteriorating. Far too many graduates lack basic verbal and cognitive abilities, and the reasons are disturbing: the disintegration of an effective core curriculum; the pervasiveness of trendy, politically correct courses that stress indoctrination over genuine learning; the dumbing down of instruction in proper writing and reasoning skills; and a growing gap between what students are taught and what they must know to succeed as teachers or other professionals.

Analyst David P. Doyle describes teacher education in these terms: "It is a classic example of a 'closed' system, one in which there is little or no feedback from the outside world. Once through the process, teachers heave a sigh of relief and get on with their work. Teacher educators, institutionally insulated, have been under little pressure to change or improve. Worse yet, their inertia is reinforced by state teacher licensing requirements that mirror the vapid courses they offer."

LOWERED STANDARDS

Let's examine a few of the dubious exercises our universities are engaged in.

Most college graduates over the age of 40 will recall taking freshman English composition. That's the course in which they learned the fundamentals of written exposition, including a review of grammar and syntax, and some lessons in informal logic and the rules of evidence. A tedious but valuable course, freshman composition once sharpened universally applicable skills that helped us deal meaningfully with material and assignments in other courses.

But in universities today, much of what passes for freshman composition is trivial and irrelevant, or worse. Heather Mac-Donald writes in *The Public Interest*, "The only thing composition teachers are not talking and writing about these days is how to teach students to compose clear, logical prose."

THE PUBLIC VERSUS THE PROFESSORS

A survey by Public Agenda, a policy research group, found that six in 10 Americans say their public schools don't place enough emphasis on the basics, such as reading, writing and math. Half the public believes the schools don't teach good work habits, and just over half say they weren't satisfied with the way teachers were dealing with discipline in the classroom.

"But ask the professors of education . . . what they seek to transmit to their student teachers, and a very different agenda emerges," Public Agenda analysts Steve Farkas, Jean Johnson and Ann Duffett reported. "Education professors put the public's priorities squarely at the bottom of their list."

Richard Morin, *Washington Post National Weekly Edition*, November 17, 1997.

Course syllabi and related materials from English departments and writing programs in universities across the country reveal a general lowering—and in some cases, an abandonment—of standards of correct writing. Self-expression and moral liberation (the "anything goes" approach) are often emphasized over prose competency. Typical is this professor's advice from a freshman composition course syllabus at Eastern Michigan University: "Don't worry about writing perfect papers. I do not have a set standard for what I consider 'good writing.'"

ARE BASIC SKILLS "ELITIST"?

Professor Bertonneau conducted a survey of the master syllabi for freshman composition at Michigan's universities. His work revealed the dominance of a school of thought that denigrates the very notion of "basic skills." According to this view, there is no connection between a knowledge of grammar, syntax, and logic on the one hand, and the communication competency of students on the other. Emphasizing basic skills is characterized as "elitist," or as an exercise in "discrimination" against ethnic minorities, or as a manifestation of an "oppressive" economic system.

A study from the Empire Foundation in the summer of 1996 showed that the same philosophy pervades the state universities of New York. Indeed, this is a cancer that afflicts higher education—and hence, teacher training—all across America.

The abandonment of rules and standards in the universities shows up in other ways too—in a popular but dubious focus on "peer teaching," for example. This is an activity in which students who have not yet gained competency in prose are supposed to substitute for the teacher and teach each other what none of them by himself knows, namely, the elements of clear and correct communication.

Dr. Peter T. Koper, one of Professor Bertonneau's colleagues at Central Michigan University, dissents from this prevailing orthodoxy. He sees the trends cited here as inherently divisive. In Koper's view, "Grammar is not elitist. It is, rather, quintessentially democratizing, the ability to use Standard Written English being the condition for participating in public life in this country and in much of the rest of the world."

A LACK OF RIGOROUS STUDY

A preference for trivia is also part of the problem in today's teacher education courses. The curricula offered by university education departments are heavy on fuzzy "self-awareness," "multicultural," and other faddish or politicized material, and light on the hard knowledge of the subjects that teachers will eventually have to teach. One assignment, offered as a model to teaching assistants at a major university, asked students to watch and discuss TV talk shows like *Oprah* and *Montel* for two weeks of a 15-week semester.

Rigorous content in the traditional liberal arts has disintegrated in favor of cultivating emotions and politically correct opinions. The result is a huge disservice to prospective teachers who pay good money to become prepared for the classroom but are instead diverted into shallow, unproductive, and even irrelevant course work. If that were the end of it, it would be tragedy enough. But millions of taxpayers who help pay the bill and millions of children who suffer at the hands of poorly prepared teachers are casualties too.

This cake was baked with ingredients that could hardly have produced any other outcome: a tax-funded, politicized education system leavened with institutionalized protection for incompetence and annual financial rewards for mediocrity.

Education reformers have scored points everywhere by painting K-12 public education as an unresponsive government institution in need of competition, accountability, even privatization. If they take a look at universities, they will find much the same thing.

PERIODICAL BIBLIOGRAPHY

The following articles have been selected to supplement the diverse views presented in this chapter. Addresses are provided for periodicals not indexed in the *Readers' Guide to Periodical Literature*, the *Alternative Press Index*, the *Social Sciences Index*, or the *Index to Legal Periodicals and Books*.

Karl L. Alexander	"Public Schools and the Public Good," *Social Forces*, September 1997.
Gerald W. Bracey	"Are U.S. Students Behind?" *American Prospect*, March/April 1998.
Carol C. Chmelynski	"Segregated Schools in the '90s," *Education Digest*, January 1998.
Lee A. Daniels	"Derailing a System," *Emerge*, September 1996. Available from One BET Plaza, 1990 W. Place NE, Washington, DC 20018-1211.
Barbara Lerner	"America's Schools: Still Failing After All These Years," *National Review*, September 15, 1997.
Tamar Lewin	"Public Schools Confronting Issue of Racial Preferences," *New York Times*, November 29, 1998.
Richard Morin	"Lessons from the Education Professors," *Washington Post National Weekly Edition*, November 17, 1997. Available from PO Box 1150, 15th St. NW, Washington, DC 20071.
New York Times	"Education Life" (entire section on education), January 3, 1999.
Policy Review	"A Nation Still at Risk," July/August 1998.
Virginia I. Postrel	"Test Case: How Relying on 'The Experts' Failed Public Education," *Reason*, February 1998.
Rosemary C. Salomone	"Common Schools, Uncommon Values: Listening to the Voices of Dissent," *Yale Law & Policy Review*, vol. 14, no. 1, 1996.
Svi Shapiro	"Public School Reform: The Mismeasure of Education," *Tikkun*, January/February 1998.
Janice Weinman and Judith Kleinfeld	"Q: Do Public Schools Shortchange Girls on Educational Opportunities?" *Insight*, December 14, 1998. Available from 3600 New York Ave. NE, Washington, DC 20002.
Ellen A. Seay Young	"A Teacher Decries Misdirected Reform," *Education Digest*, December 1997.

CHAPTER 2

SHOULD PARENTS BE ALLOWED TO CHOOSE THEIR CHILDREN'S SCHOOLS?

Chapter Preface

In most U.S. cities, a student enrolled in the public school system is assigned to a local school by the district. Parents do not usually select the public school that their child will attend. In recent years, however, a growing number of citizens have backed reformers' efforts to allow parents to choose their children's schools. Such "parental choice" alternatives include open-enrollment options, which allow parents to send their child to any public school in their state; charter schools, which are publicly funded schools run by private groups; and voucher programs, in which parents are given state-funded tuition grants to send their children to private schools.

Voucher programs stirred up controversy in the 1990s, when voters and lawmakers in more than fifteen states considered or enacted school-choice legislation. A pilot program in Wisconsin permitted both non-religious and religious private schools to accept tuition vouchers, which, according to the American Civil Liberties Union, violated "the constitutionally mandated separation of church and state." In June 1998, however, the Wisconsin Supreme Court ruled that vouchers did not infringe on church-state separation. This ruling was appealed to the U.S. Supreme Court, which voted not to hear the case, thereby allowing parochial schools to continue participating in voucher programs.

Voucher supporters argue that programs such as Wisconsin's grant low-income parents the freedom to take their children out of poorly run public schools and send them to high-quality private and parochial schools. Activist Alveda King maintains that this kind of school choice will "alleviate [educational] inequality [and] restore parents' and children's civil rights." Opponents, however, contend that voucher programs wrongly require taxpayers to finance sectarian schools that may conflict with their political and religious beliefs. As former Los Angeles teacher Leonce Gaiter puts it: "Will Jews be forced to underwrite . . . schools that hold Judaism to be a second-class religion? Will gay and lesbian Americans pay for classes teaching that they are sinners deserving of any ill that befalls them?" Other critics fear that state governments will require parochial schools to teach secular curricula that undermine religious values.

The debate over school choice will likely intensify in the twenty-first century as more states consider adopting voucher programs. The authors in the following chapter discuss the issue of vouchers and other parental-choice educational alternatives.

> "[Poor parents deserve] the same
> freedom of choice that wealthy
> parents have to decide which schools
> are best for their kids."

THE GOVERNMENT SHOULD OFFER SCHOOL TUITION VOUCHERS

Donald Lambro

Many proponents of school choice support the use of vouchers—state-funded tuition grants—that enable parents to choose private or parochial schools for their children to attend. In the following viewpoint, syndicated columnist Donald Lambro argues in support of school voucher programs. Vouchers give poor and minority parents the opportunity to send their children to high-quality schools that they otherwise could not afford. Such programs offer inner-city children the means to become well-educated and to rise out of poverty, Lambro maintains.

As you read, consider the following questions:

1. According to Lambro, which groups have fought against school choice?
2. How did Wisconsin's pilot school voucher program get started, according to the author?
3. Where does the money for Wisconsin's school voucher program come from, according to Lambro?

Reprinted from Donald Lambro, "School Choice Voucher Plans on the Rise," *Conservative Chronicle*, December 2, 1998, by permission of United Feature Syndicate, Inc.

The U.S. Supreme Court's stunning decision to allow the Wisconsin school choice program to use state funds for private and parochial schools didn't get much media attention in November 1998, but it now opens the way for similar plans across the country.

The limited Wisconsin plan, which gives state vouchers to poor Milwaukee families to help them send their kids to higher performance private schools, has been the shining centerpiece of the emerging school choice movement. But it has been fought every step of the way by the public teacher unions, the American Civil Liberties Union and the National Association for the Advancement of Colored People (NAACP), even though the program mostly benefits poor black inner city families who are trapped in one of the worst school districts in the country.

The program was spearheaded in the Wisconsin legislature by fiery state Rep. Polly Williams, a former welfare mother and Jesse Jackson ally, who persuasively argued that her mostly poor Milwaukee constituents deserved the same freedom of choice that wealthy parents have to decide which schools are best for their kids.

The state legislature agreed with her and a modest pilot program was begun several years ago to provide 1,500 children with state tuition vouchers to attend nonreligious private schools of their choice within their metropolitan area. The plan was opposed by the same liberal groups, but the courts eventually upheld it as constitutional.

The program was then expanded to permit religious schools to participate and after a series of court tests, the Wisconsin Supreme Court ruled in June 1998 that it did not violate the U.S. Constitution's separation of church and state doctrine.

A VICTORY FOR SCHOOL CHOICE

As many as 7,500 students are benefiting from the enlarged voucher plan which provides up to $4,900 to the poorest Milwaukee families. The money, which pays for tuition at 81 religious and 31 nonreligious schools in the area, comes directly out of the public school budget.

Opponents appealed to the U.S. Supreme Court, asking that the issue be taken up and decided once and for all. Their appeal was turned down without explanation. The highest court in the land voted 8–1 (only Justice Stephen Breyer dissented) not to hear the case, and thus allowed the unprecedented voucher program for both religious and nonreligious private schools alike to continue uninterrupted.

While the Supreme Court remains silent on the educational issues raised by school choice opponents, its decision not to take up the case sent a strong signal that it found no egregious violation of Constitutional principles were at stake here.

The green light for the Wisconsin plan has school choice advocates crowing and has significantly advanced their nationwide agenda for educational and social reform.

WHY THE U.S. NEEDS SCHOOL CHOICE

U.S. citizenship guarantees all parents an education for their children. This is a true civil right. Yet some children receive a better education than others due to their parents' abilities to pay for benefits that are often missing in public schools. This inequity is a violation of the civil rights of the parents and children who are so afflicted by lack of income and by the mismanagement endemic to so many of the country's public school systems.

Alveda C. King, *Wall Street Journal*, September 11, 1997.

"The court's decision removes the last hurdle for Milwaukee's most disadvantaged children to reach the lifeline of a quality education," said Pete Hutchison, the general counsel for the Landmark Legal Foundation which had urged the court to simply let the Wisconsin court ruling stand rather than to take up the case and possibly muddy the waters. The court wisely took its advice.

"The education establishment—its unions, its bureaucrats, and its ideological bedfellows—have for a decade fought this opportunity scholarship program despite overwhelming public support," Hutchison said. "The Supreme Court's action sends the signal that programs like the Milwaukee choice plan are legal."

HOPE FOR THE POOR

It is easy to understand why the plan is so popular among Polly Williams' poor black constituents, despite the NAACP's anti-choice, ideologically knee-jerk position. For the first time, dirt poor minority families are being given the same educational choices that the Clintons, the Kennedys, the Rockefellers and even the Jesse Jacksons enjoyed for their kids—the freedom to send them to the best school possible in their community. In most cases their test scores are up and many if not most of these inner city kids will go on to some form of higher education which is the surest way to rise out of poverty.

Wisconsin Gov. Tommy Thompson says that the court's decision opens the way "for impoverished families who want a better life for their children to choose schools that make the most sense to them. It's a victory for hope."

The Supreme Court's decision is not only an enormous political and social victory for upward mobility among lower income Americans, it is a devastating political defeat for the union-dominated public school monopoly whose days are numbered.

School choice voucher plans are going to be blossoming soon in state legislatures around the country. Wisconsin and Polly Williams led the way. Now it's time for the rest of the country to follow their example.

> "Vouchers are not an appropriate policy alternative to our system of universal free public education."

THE GOVERNMENT SHOULD NOT OFFER SCHOOL TUITION VOUCHERS

National Education Association

In the following viewpoint, the National Education Association (NEA) argues against school voucher programs—programs that allow parents to use state tax revenues to send their children to private schools. The NEA maintains that the use of vouchers drains needed funds away from public schools and could damage the quality of public education. Because private schools are selective and tend to choose the best students, the needy and less-advantaged students would be left behind in the under-funded public schools. Such a situation would increase, rather than decrease, educational inequality, the NEA contends. Moreover, recent studies reveal that students who receive vouchers do not significantly improve in academic achievement. The NEA is an organization of educators committed to advancing the cause of public education.

As you read, consider the following questions:
1. How many millions of dollars of state education funding did Milwaukee lose to voucher programs from 1998 to 1999, according to the NEA?
2. In the opinion of the NEA, how do vouchers make schools less accountable for education?
3. What school reforms would truly improve education for all children, in the NEA's view?

Reprinted, with permission, from "The Case Against School Vouchers," by the National Education Association, 1999.

The idea of school vouchers—using tax dollars to send children to private and religious schools—surfaced publicly in 1955, in a proposal by conservative economist Milton Friedman. At that time, vouchers were seen by many critics as an attempt to provide government funding for segregated all-white academies in the wake of the historic 1954 U.S. Supreme Court ruling, *Brown v. Board of Education*, which ruled that the doctrine of "separate but equal" public schools for black and white students was unconstitutional.

Ironically, one of the arguments put forth by voucher proponents in 1999 is that they are an appropriate alternative to America's urban public school systems, which are largely attended by poor and minority students. Regardless of their intended audience, it is the position of the National Education Association that vouchers are not an appropriate policy alternative to our system of universal free public education.

Currently, there are two publicly funded voucher programs (Milwaukee and Cleveland) and a number of privately funded voucher programs in several American cities.

The case against vouchers is based on five basic arguments:

• Vouchers do not improve student performance.

• Vouchers hurt the vast majority of students by taking money from public schools.

• Vouchers do not guarantee "choice" or "competition," because private schools do the choosing, and do not have to compete on a level playing field with public schools.

• Vouchers do not bring more accountability to education; they bring less.

• Small class sizes and other targeted reforms—not vouchers—are the answer for improving education for all children, and for minority students in particular.

VOUCHERS DO NOT IMPROVE STUDENT PERFORMANCE

The true test of any education reform is whether it improves student achievement, and both publicly funded voucher programs—Milwaukee (in effect since 1990) and Cleveland (since 1996)—have failed this test. In Milwaukee, an evaluation of the first five years of the program by University of Wisconsin–Madison Professor John Witte found no achievement differences between voucher students and Milwaukee public school students. In fact, students in Milwaukee's SAGE class-size reduction program outperformed regular public school students and voucher students in reading, and did as well in math.

In Cleveland, a state-sponsored study of the first year of the voucher program by Indiana University researchers found no significant differences in student achievement between voucher students and comparable Cleveland public school students. In the second-year study, there was no achievement difference in math, English, science, and social studies, and only a slight advantage for voucher students in language arts.

VOUCHERS HURT THE MAJORITY OF STUDENTS

It is an indisputable fact that vouchers—both public and private—drain funding from public school districts.

In 1998–99, public funding for some 6,000 voucher students resulted in a net loss of more than $22 million in state education funding for the Milwaukee public schools. In the same year, Cleveland public schools lost $9 million in state funding, plus another $10 million in administrative and transportation costs—taken largely from state funding earmarked for disadvantaged public school students.

In the Edgewood school district in San Antonio, Texas, the privately funded Horizon Scholarship program is costing that already-impoverished district an estimated $4.5 million in state funding.

Public schools are hurt by these transactions. Imagine a class of 25 students. One student leaves with a voucher. The classroom now has 24 students, but "fixed costs"—teacher salaries, maintenance, transportation, utilities—still must be paid. Those fixed costs are anywhere from 50–60 percent of a per pupil expenditure.

VOUCHERS DO NOT GUARANTEE CHOICE

Throughout recent history, the percentages of students attending public (89%) and private (11%) schools have remained essentially constant.

However, one key characteristic has always distinguished private schools from public schools: they are free to choose their students. Public schools must accept all students, regardless of race, disability, academic ability, special needs, family situation, or income level. Therefore, when voucher proponents talk about giving parents of all students the "choice" of attending private schools, they are holding out a false promise, because private schools have neither the capacity nor the desire to accept large numbers of public school students.

Voucher proponents also argue that vouchers will force public schools to improve, in order to "compete" with private schools. But competition is only fair when there is a level playing field. How can public schools compete with private schools if they cannot limit the number of students they enroll? How can they compete if they are losing resources to vouchers? The only competition will be for the best students, and just as health maintenance organizations (HMOs) put most of their efforts into attracting healthy customers, so, too, will private schools compete for the best students. It is a fact that 75% of private schools do not offer special education programs, because of their high cost. Private schools are more interested in "star" pupils than in students with special needs, or students from disadvantaged homes.

LESS ACCOUNTABILITY

If private schools receive public funding, the vast majority of Americans believe they should be accountable for how those tax dollars are spent. Yet, a 1998 study by the U.S. Department of Education indicates that private and religious schools would not be willing to participate in voucher plans that require them to meet the kinds of accountability standards that the public desires. Only 15% of private and religious schools, for example, would be "definitely or probably willing" to accept special needs students. Only 33% would be willing to use state tests, while only 36% would accept students at random.

PARENTAL CHOICE IS A MISNOMER

Private schools retain the right to reject or accept any student, regardless of whether the student holds a voucher. By definition, private schools are selective, using a variety of criteria to weed out applications. Further, most private and religious school costs would not be covered by the value of the voucher. Other voucher-eligible students find that the voucher is an illusion of choice, because no openings are available to them. For example, a September 30, 1997, *Washington Post* story disclosed that private school openings in the area are few and that tuition costs are significantly higher than the voucher subsidy.

NEA online report, June 1998.

Accountability takes a number of forms. Parents want their children's teachers to be well-trained and licensed. Yet according to the National Center for Educational Statistics, only 71% of private school teachers are licensed, compared to 97.4% of public school teachers. In addition, while all states are moving toward higher academic standards and more rigorous curricula, no state requires private schools to meet the same state curriculum standards as public schools. And when it comes to testing students, no state requires private school students to take the same tests as public school students.

Financial accountability is another concern. As noted earlier, voucher programs in Milwaukee and Cleveland have failed to enhance student performance, while costing taxpayers millions of dollars. Four Milwaukee voucher schools closed down—two because of financial fraud. In Cleveland, the voucher program was 41% over budget in 1997–98, with $1.5 million misspent on taxicabs to transport students. The city's taxpayers footed the bill for these mistakes.

If vouchers ever became a national policy, they would invite the creation of "fly by night" private schools to provide the seats that current private and religious schools do not have. There would be little or no accountability for how these new schools would spend public funds. According to the Small Business Association, 53% of all new small businesses fail within their first four years. Do we really want to invest tax dollars in unproven educational experiments?

THERE ARE BETTER CHOICES THAN VOUCHERS

It is a fact that there are public schools that are struggling, and failing to provide their students with a quality education. Most of them are in urban settings, where social and economic problems plague large numbers of families. Voucher proponents are essentially urging us to abandon those schools by letting a fraction of their students attend private and religious schools at taxpayer expense, while leaving the vast majority behind in public schools that would be weakened by declining resources.

However, those same taxpayers disagree. Public opinion polls consistently show that given the choice between taxpayer-funded vouchers and improving public schools, Americans overwhelmingly prefer improving the public schools.

There are better choices than vouchers. Smaller class sizes in grades K-3—as proven by the landmark Tennessee STAR class size project, and the current SAGE program in Milwaukee—produce higher levels of student achievement for all students, and for disadvantaged students in particular. Other programs, like Success for All, an intensive reading-based curriculum now in place in more than 1,100 schools nationwide, produce strong gains in student achievement, at a fraction of the cost of vouchers.

If our goal truly is to help provide a quality education for as many children as possible, the answer lies in proven reforms like these that are already helping large numbers of students succeed. Vouchers are not the answer, because in the end, they will only provide economic benefits to those families whose children are already in private and religious schools, at the expense of the 90% of America's children who continue to attend our public schools.

| "Catholic schools already do an outstanding job of serving the poor and minorities, and they're eager to do more."

CHOICE PROGRAMS SHOULD INCLUDE RELIGIOUS SCHOOLS

Part I: Charles J. Chaput, Part II: Reggie White and Sara White

The authors of the following two-part viewpoint contend that parents should be able to use vouchers to pay for their children's education in a religious school. In Part I, Charles J. Chaput maintains that Catholic schools are prepared to work with disadvantaged youth and should be allowed to accept voucher students. Chaput is the archbishop of Denver, Colorado. In Part II, Reggie White and Sara White argue that voucher programs that include parochial schools give parents, children, and teachers the opportunity to combine religious faith and values with education. Reggie White is a former defensive end for Wisconsin's Green Bay Packers and the NFL's all-time sack leader. Sara White, his wife, is a cofounder of Urban Hope, a ministry that serves inner-city residents. The Whites are also senior fellows with the Alexis de Tocqueville Institution, an organization that promotes economic freedom and opportunity.

As you read, consider the following questions:

1. Why did a group of African-American parents sue the Denver, Colorado, school board in 1997, according to Chaput?
2. In Chaput's opinion, why is it unlikely that school vouchers constitute a violation of the separation of church and state?
3. According to the Whites, in what ways has choice improved schools in East Harlem, New York?

"Diversity" and "choice" are words with almost sacred resonance in today's culture; they have become cornerstones of our democratic vocabulary. But some kinds of diversity and choice are less equal than others—especially when it comes to education, and most especially when it comes to educational choice.

THE NEED TO RETHINK EDUCATION

In the summer of 1997, a group of local African-American parents brought suit against the Denver public school system. Arguing that the system has failed to educate their children adequately, they're demanding that the annual budget allotted to schools for each of their children should be paid instead directly to them. They, not professional administrators, then would decide how best to disburse the funds and which schools to support with those dollars. Not surprisingly, the school district has resisted this idea, just as public schools have fought vouchers for decades.

The litigants are not ideological conservatives bent on privatizing public education, but frustrated minority families who simply want to take back one of their basic rights—the power to make decisions about how best, and where, to educate their daughters and sons.

As so often in the past, their action may bear little fruit—for now. But like a battering ram that gradually hammers through the thickest fortress wall, frustrated parents are shaking America's last great monopoly, public education, to its roots. Too many families now recognize that too many public schools, especially in the inner city, do a bad job of educating their children. The evidence for this failure in crime and illiteracy statistics is overwhelming.

What's needed in American education is not cosmetic reforms, but a systemic rethinking of how our education system is structured. We need to turn away from the monopoly model of public education. Parents are, after all, the primary educators of their children. Some form of vouchers to assist them in that responsibility is long overdue.

CATHOLIC SCHOOL SUCCESS

Schools with limited budgets can frequently produce far better results than heavily funded ones. At Loyola Catholic School in Denver's inner city, more than 80% of the students are African-American, and more than half are non-Catholic. Many struggle with poverty. But like its Catholic sister schools elsewhere in the inner city, Loyola has created a superior learning environment with active parental support. It boasts an atmosphere of positive discipline, strong moral formation and a competitive academic program. As a result, Loyola students learn not merely facts, but the mutual respect and personal pride that come from genuine achievement. Dropout rates are low. Graduation rates are high. Bureaucracies are small. And Loyola accomplishes all this at a cost of $2,500 per student, vs. $5,000 in the Denver public schools.

The outstanding performance of northern Colorado's Catholic schools—which, by the way, have 22% minority enrollment—parallels the national Catholic school record of success. The result is a growing demand for their services in Colorado—ironically, one of the least "churched" states in the nation. Total local enrollment is now greater than at any time since the mid-1980s and has grown in each of the past 11 years.

But education successes like these Catholic schools are officially discouraged by being barred from most public support. This, despite the fact that virtually all other advanced industrial democracies do provide financial aid to religious and private schools, with no damage to their political integrity. In other words, in real world experience, any church-state confusions arising from public support for religious and private schools are clearly solvable. And vouchers, which put financial power directly into the hands of parents rather than school authorities, would make church-state entanglements even less likely.

SERVING DISADVANTAGED CHILDREN

My point here is not that Catholic schools should replace government-run ones. They aren't designed to. Thousands of good teachers and administrators work hard in public education and make a positive difference for children. They deserve our gratitude and respect. Additionally, any voucher system must solve the practical problem of the extraordinary funding and programming required to educate special-needs children at the schools their parents choose.

However, Catholic schools already do an outstanding job of serving the poor and minorities, and they're eager to do more. Earlier this year, for example, Denver education activists, entrepreneurs and local corporate leaders came together to form the Seeds of Hope Charitable Trust, a Colorado partnership to raise funds for hundreds of new inner-city scholarships annually. These will enable even more economically disadvantaged children to attend Catholic schools. Other dioceses are doing the same across the country.

VOUCHERS SHOULD WIN

Too many failures in public education over too long a time have finally—and rightly—caught up with us as a culture. It's simply not credible to argue today that the U.S. Constitution is so allergic to religion that no public means can be found to help parents send their kids to Catholic and other good alternative schools. Colorado is likely to face another fierce ballot battle over vouchers; and sooner or later vouchers will win. They *should* win, because "business as usual" in public education no longer works—especially for the poor.

Yet even the best and brightest in our public education establishment seem to underestimate the gravity of the situation. Rudy Crew, chancellor of the New York City school system and an impressive educator by any standard, is quoted in a recent *New York Times Magazine* profile as saying, "We don't have a lot of time, which is why I feel this incredible urgency [for reform]. I think we have 10 years, tops, to turn the [public school] system around before the public gets fed up and begins to replace it with something else."

He may already be too late. The process has already begun.

II

Milwaukee has the nation's most extensive school-choice program, which includes vouchers to help poor parents send their children to private schools. In June 1998, the Wisconsin Supreme Court ruled that the vouchers could be used at parochial schools, a decision embraced by the primarily black and Hispanic parents who benefit from and fought for the voucher program.

CHOICE IMPROVES SCHOOLS

The evidence is clear that choice improves schools. Take for example one poor school district—located in the poor New York City neighborhood of East Harlem—that has had public-school choice since the 1980s. Student performance on reading tests, which once ranked among the worst in the city, has risen to the average. In Milwaukee, after several years in the program, third- and fourth-grade low-income kids participating in the school-choice program have reading scores three to five percentile points higher than low-income students in the public schools. Math scores are five to 12 percentile points higher for choice students.

But numbers can't describe the broad revival—educational and spiritual—that choice has helped foster. Private individuals have formed a charity called Partners Advancing Values in Education (PAVE), which provides matching grants to parents who send their children to parochial schools. PAVE has allowed Joy Allen's three children to attend the Believers in Christ Academy. "My children learn more. I think it's a better education," says Ms. Allen, a former public-school bus driver. At the public school her children attended previously, it seemed impossible to change the entrenched system. Ms. Allen says her choice school has "a better system, because it allows the parents and teachers to share values together" through prayer and faith. Now even those not in the PAVE program can enjoy such benefits through publicly-funded vouchers.

DETERMINANTS OF ACADEMIC PERFORMANCE OF MINORITY STUDENTS: CATHOLIC SCHOOLS VS. PUBLIC SCHOOLS

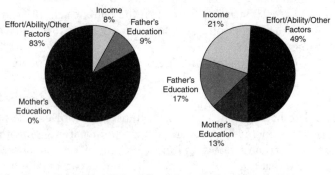

John Convey, *Catholic Schools Make a Difference: Twenty-Five Years of Research*, 1992.

Vivian Watts pulled her two boys out of public school four years ago. They now attend Resurrection Catholic Academy. Because of school choice, Ms. Watts can deal with teachers who share her religious faith and help impart it to her children. "I'm more involved now in their education and their well-being," she says.

WHY PUBLIC SCHOOLS STRUGGLE

Although public-school teachers work hard, they have little room to excel because of the mound of government and union regulations. Managing these rules requires an army of administrators and bureaucrats, which siphons precious resources away from the classrooms. An Alexis de Tocqueville Institution study has shown that the U.S. spends nearly 150% of the amount such countries as Germany and Japan do on "nonteaching personnel"—while public-school teachers' salaries, as a share of per pupil education spending, have fallen by more than 45% since 1960.

The greater availability of private school alternatives in Milwaukee has helped public schools, which must improve to keep their students from going elsewhere. The new motto of Milwaukee's public-school system: "We want to be Milwaukee's schools of choice."

PARENTAL INVOLVEMENT

Choice schools enjoy a level of parental involvement unheard of at other institutions. And much of it would be impossible in a nonchoice environment. While we were visiting Believers in Christ, a man passed by with a determined stride. "That's one of our parents—his boy is the one who did the kickoff for you in the third grade," said teacher Cheryl Brown. "He comes during his break at work to clean the toilets every day."

Choice has also given teachers more freedom to discipline children, a welcome development for parents. "I live in an apartment building with a lot of public-school kids," Ms. Allen says. "There's a difference in the children. Non-school choice kids . . . just go crazy. School choice kids are more calm."

An administrator who works on admissions for Believers in Christ told us he has seen a number of applications from parents who say they moved into the city simply to become eligible for the PAVE program. Business leaders say that school choice and the PAVE scholarships play a part in their recruitment efforts and decisions about locating plants. The existence of private-school vouchers and PAVE has resulted in many new schools opening in Milwaukee—and many more will move from the drawing board in the wake of the Wisconsin Supreme Court ruling.

Milwaukee's choice system has revived values and families in a way that can only come from religion—especially for those of us who cannot separate God from life, or faith from learning. At one elementary school, we met a child whose divorced parents couldn't even sit together peacefully one year ago. Now they are able to get along for the sake of their child. This reconciliation was made possible by a pastor who works at the school, sees the child every day and ministers to the family.

| "Vouchers will have a disastrous
effect on religious schools, which
will have no choice about which
voucher students they can accept."

RELIGIOUS SCHOOLS WILL BE
HARMED BY CHOICE PROGRAMS

Llewellyn H. Rockwell

In the following viewpoint, Llewellyn H. Rockwell argues that school voucher programs will adversely affect religious schools. Because such programs require parochial schools to randomly select students based on non-religious criteria, these schools will end up taking in undisciplined non-achievers who negatively affect the educational environment. Moreover, parochial schools will be required to offer secular curricula for non-religious students—an obligation that will undermine the teaching techniques of religious educators. Voucher programs are simply a form of welfare that will damage religious schools and impose taxes on the middle class, the author contends. Rockwell is president of the Ludwig von Mises Institute in Auburn, Alabama.

As you read, consider the following questions:

1. According to Daniel McGroarty, cited by Rockwell, what are the demographics of students in the Milwaukee school voucher program?
2. What is the purpose of religious schools, in the author's opinion?
3. In Rockwell's view, what two evils of public education are reinforced by voucher programs?

Reprinted from Llewellyn H. Rockwell, "School Vouchers: Enemy of Religion," *The Wanderer*, July 9, 1998, by permission of the author.

S upporters of school vouchers are jumping for joy over a Wisconsin Supreme Court edict that permits tax dollars to be used at religious schools. They hope that the decision will be the basis of a vast expansion of vouchers (four other states are debating this same question), eventually leading to a federal voucher program that will "privatize" all education.

But there are flies in this ointment, enough to cause religious conservatives to rethink any sympathies they've had for vouchers. For the court did not rule that religious schools can receive government money with no strings attached. It ruled narrowly on the Milwaukee program itself, which only passed muster because of its rigid restrictions. Though few will actually read the decision, it is perfectly clear that in order to receive vouchers, religious schools will have to surrender all control over admissions and gut any doctrinal teaching integral to their curricula.

FREE LUNCH FOR THE UNDERCLASS

First, let's deal with the eligibility criteria for students. The money is not available for the children of middle-class people who actually pay the taxes that support the public schools. It is available only for those whom the government defines as "poor," the very group that already enjoys vast subsidies in the form of free medical care, housing, day care, food, and cash. Vouchers represent not a shrinkage of the welfare state but an expansion, the equivalent of food stamps for private school.

What's more, vouchers are available only for children currently in public schools, which creates perverse incentives and strikes at the heart of fairness. Parents scraping by to pay their child's tuition at a parochial school get nothing, but the next-door neighbor, who lets her kid founder in the streets and the public schools, gets a full scholarship. Parents will have every incentive to rip children out of private schools and put them back into the public ones temporarily, just to be eligible for the program.

And what about middle-class kids in the private school? We know how much animosity small freebies like meals for some but not others create in public school. What about free tuition at private schools for some but not others? No matter how you slice it, vouchers represent more welfare, another free lunch for the underclass paid for by everyone else.

RANDOM ADMISSIONS

Second, vouchers will have a disastrous effect on religious schools, which will have no choice about which voucher students they can accept. Catholic schools cannot pick Catholics over Hindus. Single-sex education is out. Nor may schools consider a history of abject academic failure or even violence. In fact, the court underscored that schools are prohibited from exercising any judgment whatsoever about the students they take in (except that they may give preference to siblings). As Wisconsin Supreme Court Judge Donald J. Steinmetz, writing for the majority, said in these startling sentences, beneficiaries are to be "selected on a random basis from all those pupils who apply and meet these religious-neutral criteria." And again, "the participating private schools must select on a random basis the students attending their schools."

That's right: random admissions, somewhat like public schools. The inability to pick and choose among students, and kick out students who don't cut it in academics or discipline, is one of the reasons public schools are in trouble. Apply the same rule to private schools, especially religious schools, and you go a long way toward making them carbon copies of the schools so many are anxious to flee. Many of the recent public school shootings have been committed by students enthralled to Satanism. Voucher-taking schools would not be allowed to exclude even them.

Look at the demographics of the students in the Milwaukee program. As reported by Daniel McGroarty in the *Public Interest*, the great majority are on welfare and all are "very near the bottom in terms of academic achievement" and exhibit "a history of behavior-related problems." Do we want these kids crashing the private schools of the country at taxpayer expense? No wonder someone like Polly Williams, a black nationalist and far-leftist, is celebrating.

Undermining Religious Education

Third, regarding the religious content of the curriculum, the Wisconsin state legislature added an "opt-out" provision that prohibits a private school from requiring a student "to participate in any religious activity if the pupil's parent or guardian submits to the teacher or the private school's principal a written request that the pupil be exempt from such activities." The existence of this provision helped persuade the court that there was no violation of the U.S. Supreme Court's diktats about church and state.

But this betrays an astounding ignorance of the way many religious schools teach. There is no such thing as a "religious activity" separate from the general learning program of the school (as there might have been in public schools before the Supreme

Court prohibited even that). The very purpose of these schools is to weave religious values into the process of learning.

When these schools teach reading, among the books they select are those of Holy Scripture, and nearly all readings will have some religious lesson behind them. When these schools teach history, the history of religion is integral. When they teach art, they use religious imagery. When they teach science, they include biblical accounts of God's hand moving at the creation of the world. In these schools, the study of literature means, in part, learning about religious writing.

WHAT MAKES A SCHOOL GOOD?

Let's be honest. People (black and white) do not shun an abstraction called Public Education but its present student body, in most large cities is more than 75 percent black and Hispanic. On average, these children perform two or more grades behind whites and Asians in all academic subjects, and are far more disruptive. There is no reason to think they will miraculously become apt, obedient pupils if moved from "bad" public schools to "good" private ones. After all, what makes a school good is not its physical location, but the quality of its students and teachers.

Michael Levin, *Rothbard-Rockwell Report*, November 1996.

The court's mandate requires that the religious side of the curriculum be distinct and separate from the secular curriculum, and that the secular side be large enough to prepare students to pass standardized tests. In practice, this will require any supposed religious school to model itself on nonsectarian schools or public schools, and to do so in opposition to the parents who are shelling out tuition money precisely so that their children will have their faith reinforced.

Prayer will be allowed, so long as ample time is provided for opting-out students, even if there is only one, to leave the classroom. And can the teacher make casual reference to religious doctrine in the course of the day without first permitting opting-out students to cover their ears? And what about something as simple as a crucifix or a statue of the Blessed Mother in a classroom? Is looking at them a "religious activity"? In that case, they must be tossed out, just as they were in Catholic universities taking government money in the 1940s.

Keep in mind that this is only the first round of restrictions. Inevitably, there will be new challenges to particular practices of these religious schools, and if the courts continue in the direction they've been heading for 50 years, religion will be systematically banished. In order to avoid lawsuits, schools will err on the side of caution by voluntarily cutting the heart out of their programs.

THE DANGER OF GOVERNMENT MONEY

Knowing the implications of these "opt-out" clauses, Cardinal James Hickey of Washington, D.C., refused to allow his diocesan schools to participate in voucher programs. His refusal effectively and thankfully killed a bill in Congress that would have allocated the money.

Yet even without opt-out clauses, government money always poses a danger. Control follows tax money, so vouchers guarantee that the whole system of private education will eventually be absorbed into a gigantic government-funded propaganda machine, with the only pockets of diversity being schools that refuse any subsidies at all, though they will then be frequently outcompeted. This is precisely what happened on the university level, with a disastrous homogenization and dumbing-down.

The idea of vouchers originated on the neoconservative right with Milton Friedman, but, increasingly, the left has figured out that vouchers represent their dream come true: more special privileges for the poor, an expansion of the welfare state, the elimination of exclusive admissions, and the destruction of anachronisms like schools that still teach religious truth. We face an unholy alliance of big-government libertarians and equality activists of all stripes to rob us of what remains of educational freedom, and to do so in the name of serving up ever more of our tax dollars to the underclass.

Meanwhile, the advocates of vouchers are busy trampling on decades of conservative attacks on the notion of a "right to a quality education," which is a slogan of the left now recklessly tossed around by the Institute for Justice and the rest of the Beltway cabal. But be aware that the language of voucher supporters is drawn from an alien tradition that has no regard for limiting power and protecting property, and no appreciation for the natural inequalities of social position that are an inherent part of a free society. Truly to equalize educational opportunity would require yet another massive round of judicial activism to override neighborhood, town, and state jurisdiction, as well as the distinctions between producers and nonproducers, which is apparently what the leaders of the voucher movement advocate.

We are seldom spared the tyranny of the judiciary imposed on us by leftist egalitarians, who think nothing of robbing us and abolishing our right to self-government. Must we also suffer this fate at the hands of left-libertarians and neoconservatives stupefied by egalitarian fantasies of state-subsidized racial uplift? Not if the people have anything to say about it. Proposition 174 in California, a model piece of voucher legislation backed by all the usual suspects, crashed and burned at the polls for the very reasons laid out here. But now the activists are cheering on the courts to destroy private schools, and what's left of decent public schools, at our expense.

PUBLIC EDUCATION'S TWIN EVILS

Just as bad, vouchers reinforce the twin evils of public education: involuntary funding and compulsory attendance. As Mark Brandly of Ball State University has pointed out, compulsory attendance laws not only violate parental rights, they allow government to define what a school is, and therefore to outlaw such developments as small, informal neighborhood schools, held in homes, in which one mother teaches arithmetic, another reading, another Christian doctrine, and so on. Yet today, such alternative schools are illegal. Vouchers do nothing to end that oppressive situation, and, in fact, go in the opposite direction: toward more draconian regulation and attempted abolition of religious education.

Religious conservatives need a more radical agenda. Get the anti-Christian federal government out of education, and cut federal taxes drastically, so parents can keep more of their own money. Eliminate the taxes that now fund the anti-Christian public-education industry at the state level, and keep all taxes and decision-making at the local level. The ultimate goal must be entirely private education.

Government is always in competition with God, since it wants children trained to worship it. As for private and especially religious schools, including home schools and cooperative groups of home schools, we must oppose any restrictions whatsoever. The push for vouchers is not only a distraction from this urgent agenda; it is destructionism masquerading as freedom.

| "We [charter schools] can flunk kids who aren't ready to pass. We can fire a teacher who just isn't performing. Try doing that in a regular school."

CHARTER SCHOOLS ARE BENEFICIAL

Jeff Jacoby

Charter schools are state-funded public institutions that are not administered by local school districts. They are sponsored by autonomous groups, such as nonprofit organizations or groups of parents, who want more control over the educational process. In the following viewpoint, syndicated columnist Jeff Jacoby argues in support of charter schools. He contends that such schools offer a public-education alternative to parents who want their children to experience high-quality, rigorous instruction.

As you read, consider the following questions:

1. According to Jacoby, why were the founders of the proposed North Bridge Classical Charter School dissatisfied with public education?
2. How many children are currently enrolled in charter schools, according to the author?
3. In Jacoby's opinion, in what way are charter schools a "return to education as it was known?"

Reprinted from Jeff Jacoby, "Charter Schools Offer 'a Ray of Hope,'" *Conservative Chronicle*, March 4, 1998, by permission of the author.

They don't look like relics from the 19th century. Sitting in Pam and Tony D'Ambrosio's living room on a frigid New England night, the founding parents of the proposed North Bridge Classical Charter School seem altogether . . . normal. Among the group of 17 parents hoping to start a new charter school in the northwest suburbs of Boston in 1999 are soccer moms and medical engineers, a karate instructor and a corporate attorney, a mutual fund manager and a physician, the head of human resources for a pharmaceutical firm and a software whiz. Nearly all these parents have college degrees; several have two or three.

But as any teachers union official or superintendent of schools would no doubt be glad to tell you, these modern, educated, suburban parents are actually backward-looking reactionaries. Their ideas about education are hopelessly archaic. If the Commonwealth of Massachusetts grants them the charter they are seeking, there is no telling what kind of mischief they'll cause.

Just listen to them.

THE PROBLEM WITH PUBLIC SCHOOLS

"Classrooms shouldn't be social gatherings," Lee Ann Kay of Concord is saying. "In our school, students will sit in desks, organized in rows, all facing the same way, with the teacher at the head of the room." Needless to say, this flies in the face of modern pedagogical theory, which holds that students should be dispersed into scattered circles, discussing their lessons in small groups while the teacher strolls from one to another like the hostess of a cocktail party. Rows of desks, faces forward? What an antiquated idea.

Frank Feda, a father from nearby Maynard, voices other antiquated notions. "We won't be under the same constraints as regular public schools," he explains, "so we'll be able to make tough choices. We can flunk kids who aren't ready to pass. We can fire a teacher who just isn't performing. Try doing that in a regular school."

In the summer of 1997, most of these parents didn't know each other. What brought them together was desperation at the state of public education in their towns. All of them had been deeply involved in their children's schools. They had worked as classroom or library volunteers, run for school committee, participated in parent-teacher organizations.

But the more they saw, the less they liked. The schools lacked discipline but had plenty of sex education. The teachers were more obsessed with "self-esteem" than with academics. Lesson plans were emphatic in their political correctness but didn't stress spelling correctness.

Gradually, desperation jelled into resolve. The parents decided to compete for one of the 12 school charters to be issued in Massachusetts in 1998. Their goal: to build the kind of school that used to be commonplace in America—one providing a rigorous, traditional, fact-based education grounded in cultural literacy and moral character.

A Fast-Growing Movement

Applying for a charter is easier said than done. It took the parents hundreds of hours of research, calculation, and consultation—all on their own time and at their own expense. In January 1998 they submitted a proposal, blunt and blessedly jargon-free, to the state department of education. They will soon learn whether they made the final cut.

As word has spread of the type of school the North Bridge parents are planning, hundreds of families have signaled an interest. No surprise: Charter schools are the fastest-growing educational movement in America. In 1992 there was one such school; today there are more than 800, with an enrollment of more than 200,000 students—and tens of thousands waiting to get in.

In some states, such as Michigan, so many parents have opted to send their children to charter schools that local officials have been reduced to begging parents to reconsider. In Mesa, Ariz., where 20 charter schools have enrolled more than 5,000 students, the school district has been running ads to try and win some of them back.

In Support of Charter Schools

Most charter schools are not for profit, receiving equivalent state funds per pupil for the students they recruit. At their best, they emulate the vigorous spirit of successful professional firms, from law to accounting to landscape architecture. That means a cadre of people with enthusiasm for the challenge, dependence on each other for success, and a passion for staying ahead.

That's what we owe our children.

Neal Peirce, *Liberal Opinion Week*, November 11, 1996.

But too many parents are beyond wooing. For all the hundreds of billions of dollars being poured into "education reform," they have lost hope that the regular public schools can be reformed. They want what the North Bridge parents want: Schools that operate the way schools used to operate. No funky educational theory. No gibberish about "higher-order learning skills." No "whole math" that doesn't use numbers. No reading without phonics.

Supporting Classical Education

What the North Bridge parents have in mind for their students is a truly classical education, right down to penmanship, daily assemblies, Latin—and a belief not only in excellence, but in excellence that can be measured. "It worked for our parents," remarks Amy Contrada, who studied violin at Oberlin and now raises two kids in Acton, Mass. "Why wouldn't it work for our children?"

The scene in the D'Ambrosios' living room is being mirrored all over the country. It presages the end of public education as we know it, and a return to education as it was known. Whether this particular group of reformers gets its charter is almost beside the point. "There are so many other parents who are equally frustrated," Contrada says. "We run into them all the time. We want them to know they're not alone. They might be up against these big, gray school bureaucracies, but they have to know they're not alone.

"This seemed like such a ray of hope. We figured we'd give it a try."

| "Charter schools are not the panacea their supporters make them out to be."

CHARTER SCHOOLS MAY BE HARMFUL

Gary Orfield

Charter schools are not necessarily a good alternative to regular public schools, argues Gary Orfield in the following viewpoint. Charter schools—publicly funded schools operated by non-government groups—are often mismanaged and are subject to the political and sectarian biases of the groups that run them. Moreover, the author contends, some charter schools have failed to improve students' academic performance. Orfield maintains that the use of alternatives within the public school system—such as magnet schools—is preferable to the risks associated with charter schools. Orfield is a professor of education and social policy at Harvard University.

As you read, consider the following questions:

1. According to Orfield, how many charter schools were operating in early 1997?
2. In what ways do charter schools limit choices, in Orfield's opinion?
3. What is the "small-school movement," according to the author?

The charter school movement has swept the country, offering what many say is a simple, low-cost answer to the educational crisis. If bureaucracy and rigidity are to blame for failing schools, then why not contract groups of educators and businesses to run their own schools, using public money?

Well, it's not that simple. Charter schools are not the panacea their supporters make them out to be. Indeed, these schools are not well regulated and often fail to serve students or their communities fairly or well. Furthermore, the flexibility and innovation ideally offered by charter schools can be achieved with fewer risks within public school systems.

MISGUIDED SUPPORT FOR CHARTER SCHOOLS

Advocates of charter schools, like Lisa Graham Keegan, Arizona's Superintendent of Education, stress that charters upgrade educational standards by forcing schools to compete against one another and by attracting new players who can provide new and challenging environments for learning.

Since 1991, when a Minnesota law pioneered state charters, such schools have grown in popularity. There were 252 operating in the 1995–1996 school year; there were 428 by early 1997.

Support for charter schools comes from high places and cuts across party lines. President George Bush favored charter schools. So does President Bill Clinton. In 1997 he proposed doubling the charter school budget, and the Republican-controlled Congress approved an increase of almost 60 percent.

This support is misplaced. A charter, after all, is not an educational program. It is a school that uses public money to advance a privately defined vision of education. In one school that vision may be a positive plan put into place by dedicated teachers. In another, a biased or sectarian group may have a disturbing agenda.

In July 1997, for instance, the Los Angeles school board narrowly avoided granting a charter to Scientologists who failed to disclose their religious orientation in their application and who planned to include the writings of L. Ron Hubbard in the curriculum. The charter was blocked, but almost by chance—a school board member and local reporters investigated rumors about the applicants' backgrounds and beliefs.

In Michigan, charter schools have misused public money. One school bought equipment, furniture and supplies without first soliciting competitive bids as required by state law. Another spent more than $500,000, nearly half its budget, on illegal building renovations.

And in Arizona, Lisa Keegan's own state, numerous schools

lost their charters because of questionable fiscal dealings by the officials running them.

Of course, problems exist in public schools as well. But at least there are more systems in place to detect corruption or unapproved curriculums. Renegade charter schools would be much harder to rein in.

CHARTER SCHOOLS LIMIT CHOICES

Although charter schools are required to obey the same Federal regulations that apply to public schools, recent research shows that some do not provide for disabled children, while others ignore the rights of students who need instruction in English as a second language.

Some charters limit choices even as they appear to offer them. In theory, students can choose to enroll in a particular charter school as long as there is space. In reality, those lacking their own means of transportation are at the mercy of mass transit, which is not always available. As a result, charter schools in affluent neighborhoods remain inaccessible to poor and disadvantaged children.

STOP FUNDING UNPROVEN EXPERIMENTS

The public, especially in tax-weary states like New York, has grown tired, even skeptical, of the incessant pleas by educators for more money. In such a climate, New York City Schools Chancellor Rudy Crew's perspective is one that resonates widely: public financing for alternative public institutions like charter schools, or for private schools, is financing being denied to the very schools the public has created and held accountable.

If it can be granted that financing for education has limits, then it is in the public's interest to strengthen its existing public institutions before expending scarce public dollars on unproven experiments like charter schools.

Roger W. Bowen, New York Times, January 13, 1999.

Charter schools in the inner city are also beset with troubles. According to a 1997 study by The Detroit Free Press, test scores at some charters in high-poverty neighborhoods in Michigan were very low, with the Detroit schools performing below the city's already substandard average. Vaughn Next Century School, a charter school in Los Angeles praised by President Clinton, reported in 1997 that scores fell below the 30th percentile on standard tests used by all Los Angeles schools. These children might have been better served had they been able to transfer to good suburban or magnet schools.

PUBLIC SCHOOL ALTERNATIVES

This leads to the most important reason that the emphasis on charter schools is misplaced. Their aims can be realized within public school districts.

Magnet schools, for example, have been in operation for more than 20 years and offer many of the same possibilities as charters but more equitably and on a larger scale. Most of these schools provide transportation for students who can't get there themselves. And magnet schools are usually committed to voluntary desegregation.

Another alternative is the small-school movement, which calls for unsuccessful larger schools to be broken up into a number of innovative smaller schools. The idea has been successful in New York City and elsewhere.

Still another success has been the reconstitution process, pioneered in 1983 in an African-American neighborhood of San Francisco. This program emptied out failing schools and brought in energetic new staff members. They created new schools within old buildings that students from other areas of the city were eager to attend.

Of course, success stories like these don't guarantee the equal distribution of educational opportunity that our public school system sorely needs. But these approaches at least permit major reforms without the risks or the limitations of the charter process.

"Homeschooling is working . . .
surprisingly well for the growing
number of parents and children who
choose it."

HOMESCHOOLING IS VIABLE

Lawrence W. Reed

A growing number of parents are choosing to educate their
children at home. In the following viewpoint, Lawrence W. Reed
maintains that homeschooling is a feasible option for dedicated
parents who want to ensure a quality education for their children. He reports that homeschooled children score much higher
than average on standardized tests and college entrance exams;
they also grow up to become hard-working, upstanding citizens. Reed is president of the Mackinac Center for Public Policy,
a free-market research and educational organization based in
Midland, Michigan.

As you read, consider the following questions:
1. Nationwide, how many children are enrolled in
   homeschools, according to Reed?
2. For what reasons do parents choose to homeschool,
   according to the author?
3. Which recent technological innovations are likely to make
   homeschooling more attractive to parents, in Reed's opinion?

Reprinted from Lawrence W. Reed, "Homeschool Heroes," *The Freeman*, February 1997,
by permission of *The Freeman*.

Of all the ingredients in the recipe for education, which one has the greatest potential to improve student performance? No doubt the teachers unions would put higher salaries for their members at the top of the list, to which almost every reformer might reply, "Been there, done that." Teacher compensation has soared in recent decades at the same time every indicator of student performance has plummeted.

Other answers include smaller class size, a longer school year, more money for computers, or simply more money for fill-in-the-blank. The consensus of hundreds of studies over the past several years is that these factors exhibit either no positive correlation with better student performance or show only a weak connection. On this important question, the verdict is in and it is definitive: *The one ingredient that makes the most difference in how well and how much children learn is parental involvement.*

THE NEED FOR PARENTAL INVOLVEMENT

When parents take a personal interest in the education of their children, several things happen. The child gets a strong message that education is important to success in life; it isn't something that parents dump in someone else's lap. Caring, involved parents usually instill a love of learning in their children—a love that translates into a sense of pride and achievement as knowledge is accumulated and put to good use. Time spent with books goes up and time wasted in the streets goes down.

American parents were once responsible for educating their children. Until the late nineteenth century, the home, the church, and a small nearby school were the primary centers of learning for the great majority of Americans.

In more recent times, many American parents have largely abdicated this responsibility, in favor of the "experts" in the compulsory public school system. According to a 1996 report from Temple University in Pennsylvania, "nearly one in three parents is seriously disengaged from their children's education." The Temple researchers found that about one-sixth of all students believe their parents don't care whether they earn good grades and nearly one-third say their parents have no idea how they are doing in school.

HOMESCHOOL HEROES

Amid the sorry state of American education today are heroes who are rescuing children in a profoundly personal way. They are the homeschoolers—parents who sacrifice time and income to teach their children themselves. Homeschooling is the ultimate in parental involvement.

Teaching children at home isn't for everyone and no one advocates that every parent try it. There are plenty of good schools—many private and some public—that are doing a better job than some parents could do for their own children. But the fact is that homeschooling is working—and working surprisingly well—for the growing number of parents and children who choose it. That fact is all the more remarkable when one considers that these dedicated parents must juggle teaching with all the other demands and chores of modern life. Also, they get little or nothing back from what they pay in taxes for a public system they don't patronize.

While about 46 million children attend public schools and more than 5 million attend private schools, estimates of the number of children in homeschools nationwide range from 900,000 to 1.2 million. That's a comparatively small number, but it's up from a mere 15,000 in the early 1980s. In fact, homeschool enrollment has been growing by an astounding 25 percent annually for several years.

Parents who homeschool do so for a variety of reasons. Some want a strong moral or religious emphasis in their children's education. Others are fleeing unsafe public schools or schools where discipline and academics have taken a backseat to fuzzy "feel-good" or politically correct dogma. Many homeschool parents complain about the pervasiveness in public schools of trendy instructional methods that border on pedagogical malpractice.

Homeschool parents are fiercely protective of their constitutional right to educate their children. In early 1994, the House of Representatives voted to mandate that all teachers—including parents in the home—acquire state certification in the subjects they teach. A massive campaign of letters, phone calls, and faxes from homeschoolers produced one of the most stunning turnabouts in legislative history: By a vote of 424 to 1, the House reversed itself and then approved an amendment that affirmed the rights and independence of homeschool parents.

THE SUCCESS OF HOMESCHOOLING

Critics have long harbored a jaundiced view of parents who educate children at home. They argue that children need the guidance of professionals and the social interaction that come from being with a class of others. Homeschooled children, these critics say, will be socially and academically stunted by the confines of the home. But the facts suggest otherwise.

A 1990 report by the National Home Education Research Institute showed that homeschooled children score in the 80th percentile or higher, meaning that they scored better than 80 percent of other students in math, reading, science, language, and social studies. Reports from state after state show homeschoolers scoring significantly better than the norm on college entrance examinations. Prestigious universities, including Harvard and Yale, accept homeschooled children eagerly and often. And there's simply no evidence that homeschooled children (with a rare exception) make anything but fine, solid citizens who respect others and work hard as adults.

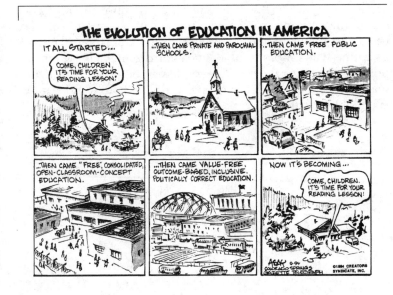

Reprinted by permission of Chuck Asay and Creators Syndicate.

Homeschool parents approach their task in a variety of ways. While some discover texts and methods as they go, others plan their work well before they start, often assisted by other homeschoolers or associations that have sprung up to aid those who choose this option. Common to every homeschool parent is the belief that the education of their children is too important to hand over to someone else.

Recent Innovations

Writing in the July 1996 issue of *Reason* magazine, Britton Manasco argues that the growth of CD-ROMs, Internet services, and computerized educational networks is likely to make homeschooling even more attractive to parents. For a tiny fraction of what a printed version might cost, one software publisher is offering a classic books program that incorporates more than 3,500 unabridged literary works, complete with hundreds of video clips and illustrations. A support group in Ann Arbor, Michigan, provides inexpensive on-line help, resources, and evaluations for thousands of homeschool children worldwide. Another organization links first-rate instructors and homeschool students from all over the country via computer in a college preparatory program that includes a core curriculum for about $250 per course.

In every other walk of life, Americans traditionally regard as heroes the men and women who meet challenges head-on, who go against the grain and persevere to bring a dream to fruition. At a time when more troubles and shortcomings plague education and educational heroes are too few in number, recognizing the homeschool heroes in our midst may be both long overdue and highly instructive.

| "Well-meaning [homeschoolers] who lack the know-how, time, or resources to be effective teachers . . . [may] deprive their children of needed social skills and a decent education."

HOMESCHOOLING MAY NOT BE VIABLE

Katherine Pfleger

Parents who choose to homeschool could be doing their children a disservice, argues Katherine Pfleger in the following viewpoint. Parents may not have the skills or resources that would enable them to give their children a high-quality, well-rounded education. Moreover, much of the research that claims that homeschooled children score higher than average on tests is statistically flawed. Pfleger concludes that the public should learn more about the potential drawbacks of homeschooling—such as the need for remedial public education of poorly homeschooled students. Pfleger is an assistant editor of the weekly magazine *New Republic*.

As you read, consider the following questions:

1. Why is school principal Carole Kennedy, quoted by Pfleger, concerned about homeschooling?
2. According to the author, why has homeschooling become increasingly popular among parents?
3. Why is the homeschooling study sponsored by the National Home Education Research Institute flawed, according to Pfleger?

Reprinted from Katherine Pfleger, "Does Homeschooling Make the Grade? School's Out," *The New Republic*, April 6, 1998, by permission of *The New Republic*. Copyright ©1998 The New Republic, Inc.

C arole Kennedy is a principal at one of the local schools in Columbia, Missouri. But one of the students she says worries her the most isn't even enrolled there. "This boy was in our school in the fourth and fifth grade and had behavior problems. His parents never had an interest in his education. They'd miss parent-teacher conferences. They'd drop him off at concerts and then not pick him up. When he got to middle school, he had attendance problems. His parents got tired of the calls from the attendance office and announced that they were going to pull him out of school and teach him at home." Homeschooling laws vary widely from state to state—some require that parents follow an approved curriculum or bring in their children for annual testing. But, in Missouri, all the boy's parents have to do is file some paperwork. "Now," says Kennedy, "his former friends say he's doing nothing all day."

HOMESCHOOLING'S INCREASING POPULARITY

Stories like this may not be as rare as we'd like to imagine. Once a relatively limited phenomenon, homeschooling is on the rise. Between 1990 and 1995 the number of children taught at home more than doubled—today it stands at over one million. And, as the popularity of homeschooling continues to increase, so does the likelihood that well-meaning parents who lack the know-how, time, or resources to be effective teachers—or, worse, parents who actually have malign motives for keeping their kids out of school—will deprive their children of needed social skills and a decent education.

Homeschooling used to be the province of the religious right. During the 1980s, Christian conservatives seized on it as a way to insulate their children from what they perceived to be the anti-family culture of public schools. These parents, generally full-time mothers, relied on religious groups to provide them with a curriculum and contacts with other homeschooling families. But, over the past few years, homeschooling has spread well beyond the Christian right; a multitude of Muslim, Jewish, African American, secular, and other homeschooling organizations are popping up across the country. And homeschooling has become an increasingly respected option. Between 1985 and 1997, the percentage of Americans who said they approved of it increased from 16 to 36 percent. Homeschooling, in short, has gone mainstream.

WHY PARENTS CHOOSE TO HOMESCHOOL

What accounts for the trend? In some cases parents see homeschooling as a remedy for the overcrowded classrooms, cookie-cutter curricula, and indifferent teachers that plague so many public school systems. In other cases parents don't trust the public schools to educate their little geniuses, or perhaps they have a child who has been diagnosed with a learning disability and want to customize his education to meet his needs. Private schooling used to be the solution to many of these problems. But, at just a couple of hundred dollars a year for texts and learning materials, homeschooling is a better bargain.

HOME SCHOOLING'S CRITICS

Critics of home schooling include many liberals and educators, as well as some education groups such as the National Education Association (NEA), a teachers' union. Opponents worry that a child who is educated only by his or her parents will lack the social skills that students learn by interacting with their peers at school. They defend traditional schools as places where children of all races and classes learn to interact, cooperate and develop the interpersonal skills that are essential for achieving success and being comfortable in the world. Some are also concerned that not all parents who home school are qualified to teach the spectrum of subjects that children need to learn before they go to college or enter the workplace. Others argue that in order to gain a full education, students need to be exposed to a variety of viewpoints and educational ideas, not just those of their parents.

Issues and Controversies on File, May 16, 1997.

And, to be sure, homeschooling is not necessarily a prescription for domestic disaster. In fact, there are some stunning success stories. Take Andy of Washington, D.C., who is marching through the fourth-grade curriculum of the Calvert School in Baltimore— one of several reputable correspondence schools that offer grades, transcripts, and diplomas to homeschoolers. Andy is a sweet and highly social kid. He participates in a chess club, arts-and-crafts classes, and group field trips. He has studied the stock market and Latin. He is fascinated by idioms. All this, at seven years old.

THE NEED FOR MORE CRITICAL SCRUTINY

But, while homeschooling enthusiasts insist that children taught at home score higher on tests and get into better colleges, a closer look at the research suggests there is little evidence either way. What few studies have been done may be flawed. The most commonly cited study, sponsored by the National Home Education Research Institute, is a case in point. According to that report, the average public school student scores in the 50th percentile on national tests, while the average homeschooler scores in the 80th to 87th percentile—regardless of race. That sounds like an open-and-shut case for homeschooling. But Glen Cutlip, an official of the National Education Association, points out that the study averages percentiles from several different tests, comparing the scores of homeschoolers nationwide with those of public school students from only the state of Virginia. In addition, he says, since the homeschoolers were selected by sending out a questionnaire, they constitute a self-selected group, not a representative sample of the entire homeschooling population.

And there's the rub. In order to assess homeschooling's effectiveness, researchers need full access to homeschooled children. Unfortunately, many homeschooling parents—particularly those in the religious right, who are also the most organized group within the movement—are vehemently opposed to any outside interference. They even have a lobby, part of the 50,000-member Home School Legal Defense Association, dedicated to blocking the logical next step that would follow further studies: the creation of national standards that would ensure all homeschooled kids are getting at least a rudimentary education.

Not that the homeschoolers need to worry about a serious challenge to their autonomy. The Department of Education has traditionally left the administration of compulsory education to local government, and it shows no inclination to get involved now. As for the press, it has been too busy touting homeschooling miracles to look at the movement critically. But, instead of glowing descriptions of seven-year-old prodigies, the public needs to hear about the overextended mothers, like the one I interviewed, while she juggled a telephone, a toddler screaming for a piece of string cheese, and a second-grader she was supposed to be homeschooling. And the public needs to hear about the public school teachers, like several in the Missouri school, who, Carole Kennedy says, are struggling to reeducate a student who fell several grades behind during the two years his mother taught him at home. This child's remedial education will cost the taxpayers money. That, if nothing else, should get the public's attention.

Periodical Bibliography

The following articles have been selected to supplement the diverse views presented in this chapter. Addresses are provided for periodicals not indexed in the *Readers' Guide to Periodical Literature*, the *Alternative Press Index*, the *Social Sciences Index*, or the *Index to Legal Periodicals and Books*.

William J. Bennett	"School Reform: What Remains to Be Done," *Wall Street Journal*, September 2, 1997.
Roger W. Bowen	"Charter Schools, Then What?" *New York Times*, January 13, 1999.
Larry and Susan Caseman	"Identifying, Celebrating, and Building on the Strengths of the Homeschooling Movement," *Home Education Magazine*, November/December 1996. Available from Home Education Press, PO Box 1083, Tonasket, WA, 98855.
Chester E. Finn and Bruno V. Manno	"Charter Schools: A New Form of Public Education," *Current*, December 1998.
Leonce Gaiter	"School Vouchers Spit in the Eye of Our Democratic Principles," *Los Angeles Times*, February 4, 1996. Available from Reprints, Times Mirror Square, Los Angeles, CA 90053.
Dan D. Goldhaber	"School Choice as Education Reform," *Phi Delta Kappan*, October 1997.
Daniel McGroarty and Nadine Strossen	"Symposium: Are School-Voucher Programs for Parochial Schools a Good Idea?" *Insight*, August 12, 1996. Available from 3600 New York Ave. NE, Washington, DC 20002.
Robert Emmet Moffit	"The Emerging Choice Option in Education," *World & I*, October 1996. Available from 3600 New York Ave. NE, Washington, DC 20002.
Salim Muwakkil	"School Choice: Do Vouchers Help or Harm Black Children?" *In These Times*, January 11, 1998.
Nina Shokraii	"Free at Last: Black America Signs Up for School Choice," *Policy Review*, November/December 1996.
David Stratman	"School Reform and the Attack on Public Education," *Dollars and Sense*, March 13, 1998.
Thomas Toch et al.	"Will Teachers Save Public Schools?" *U.S. News & World Report*, July 20, 1998.
Juliet Ucelli	"The Battle for Public Education Is On!" *Forward Motion*, Spring 1996.

CHAPTER 3

ARE MULTICULTURAL APPROACHES GOOD FOR EDUCATION?

Chapter Preface

Population analysts predict that there will be no majority race in the United States by the year 2010. This demographic shift, many educators argue, makes it imperative for today's students to learn to function in culturally diverse environments. One goal of multicultural education is to foster acceptance of diversity by increasing students' awareness of the histories and traditions of America's many racial and ethnic groups.

Supporters of multicultural education often contend that minority perspectives and realities have been excluded from the study of history, literature, and the humanities. Such exclusion leads students to wrongly conclude that civilization is the product of European males and their white descendants. This ignorance of the multiethnic nature of history intensifies intolerance and stifles moral and intellectual development, multiculturalists argue. With the purposeful inclusion of minority and female viewpoints in school curricula and textbooks, they maintain, teachers can help students broaden their perspectives and, ultimately, contribute to the common good. In the opinion of educator James A. Banks, multicultural education "helps students transcend their cultural boundaries and acquire the knowledge, attitudes, and skills needed to engage in public discourse with people who differ from themselves and to participate in the creation of a civic culture."

Critics, on the other hand, argue that multicultural education is divisive because it de-emphasizes Americans' common heritage and highlights differences based on race, class, and gender. The focus on such differences in school texts and curricula, they maintain, usually results in a shallow exposure to culturally diverse subject matter rather than an in-depth study of significant works and events. Such a superficial approach to education leaves students with little or no critical thinking abilities. Moreover, some analysts assert, multiculturalism often functions as a means to indoctrinate students into left-wing political ideologies. According to former college instructor Thomas J. Famularo, "the call for diversity in education too often . . . is a red herring for a radical agenda." Education should be free of ethnic divisiveness and political agendas, these critics contend.

Educators and activists continue to strongly disagree about the need for multicultural approaches to education. The authors in the following chapter present differing viewpoints on the hotly contested topic of multiculturalism and diversity in education.

"Multicultural education is trying to help unify a deeply divided nation, not to divide one that is united."

MULTICULTURAL EDUCATION IS BENEFICIAL

Part I: James A. Banks, Part II: Gena Dagel Caponi

The authors of the following two-part viewpoint argue that multicultural education—an education that reflects the experiences of a nation across its racial, gender, and socioeconomic boundaries—benefits all students. In Part I, James A. Banks contends that multicultural education gives students from various backgrounds the skills necessary to work in and contribute to a culturally diverse society. Schools must incorporate culturally informed teaching strategies to make high-quality education available to all students, he maintains. In Part II, Gena Dagel Caponi argues that multicultural courses broaden student perspectives and increase students' respect for cultures other than their own. Banks is professor and director of the Center for Multicultural Education at the University of Washington in Seattle. Caponi is associate professor of American Studies at the University of Texas in San Antonio.

As you read, consider the following questions:

1. According to Renato Rosaldo, cited by Banks, what is cultural citizenship?
2. In the year 2020, what percentage of the school-age population will be composed of students of color, according to Banks?
3. What are the benefits of courses that focus on specific minority groups, in Caponi's opinion?

Part I: Reprinted from James A. Banks, "Multicultural Education in the New Century," *School Administrator*, May 1999, with permission. Part II: Reprinted from Gena Dagel Caponi, "Multicultural Studies Don't Divide Us," *The Christian Science Monitor*, January 6, 1997, by permission of the author.

I

An important goal of multicultural education is to educate citizens who can participate successfully in the workforce and take action in the civic community to help the nation actualize its democratic ideals. These ideals, such as justice, equality and freedom, are set forth in the Declaration of Independence, the U.S. Constitution and the Bill of Rights.

Democratic societies, such as the United States, are works in progress that require citizens who are committed to democratic ideals, who are keenly aware of the gap between a nation's ideals and realities and who are able and willing to take thoughtful action that will help make democratic ideals a reality.

DISTORTION BY CRITICS

Although some critics have misrepresented multicultural education and argued it is divisive and will Balkanize the nation, the aim of multicultural education is to unify our nation and to help put in place its ideal of *e pluribus unum*—"out of many, one."

The claim by conservative social commentators that multicultural education will divide the nation assumes that it is now united. However, our nation is deeply divided along racial, ethnic and social-class lines. Multicultural education is trying to help unify a deeply divided nation, not to divide one that is united.

Multicultural theorists assume that we cannot unite the nation around its democratic ideals by forcing people from different racial, ethnic and cultural groups to leave their cultures and languages at the schoolhouse door. An important principle of a democratic society is that citizens will voluntarily participate in the commonwealth and that their participation will enrich the nation-state.

When citizens participate in society and bring their cultural strengths to the national civic culture, both they and the nation are enriched. Renato Rosaldo, the Stanford anthropologist, calls this kind of civic participation *cultural citizenship*.

We can create an inclusive, democratic and civic national community only when we change the center to make it more inclusive and reflective of the diversity that enriches our nation. This will require that we bring people and groups that are now on the margins of society into the center.

Schools should be model communities that mirror the kind of democratic society we envision. In democratic schools the curriculum reflects the cultures of the diverse groups within society, the languages and dialects that students speak are respected and valued, cooperation rather than competition is fostered among students and students from diverse racial, ethnic and social-class groups are given equal status in the school.

MAJOR CHALLENGES

Several societal trends present challenges for educating effective citizens in the new century. These trends include the growing ethnic, racial, cultural and language diversity in the United States, caused in part by the largest influx of immigrants to the nation since the beginning of the 20th century.

Unlike in the past, most immigrants are coming from nations in Asia and Latin America. Only a small percentage of the immigrants are coming from European nations. U.S. Census projections indicate that people of color will make up 47.5 percent of the nation's population by 2050. Students of color will make up about 48 percent of the nation's school-age youth by 2020. In 1995, they made up 35 percent of the nation's public school students.

The increasing percentage of school-age youth who speak a first language other than English and the widening gap between the rich and poor also present challenges to educating effective citizens in the new century. In 1990, 14 percent of school-age youth spoke a first language other than English. One in every five was living below the official government poverty line.

The challenge to school leaders is to find ways to ensure that the rich contributions that diverse groups can make to our nation and the public schools becomes a reality. The cultural and language groups within our nation have values, perspectives and languages that can help the nation solve some of its intractable problems and humanize the lives of all of its citizens. During World War II the lives of many American soldiers were saved because the Navajo language was used in a secret code that perplexed military leaders in Japan. The code contributed to the victory of the Allies in the South Pacific and also was used in the Korean and Vietnam wars.

In order for multicultural education to be implemented in ways that will help actualize effective citizenship education, improve race relations and increase the academic achievement of students from diverse groups, the field must be viewed broadly and attention must be paid to the research that has accumulated during the last two decades. This research, briefly summarized below, is reviewed extensively in the *Handbook of Research on Multicultural Education.*

Too often multicultural education is conceptualized narrowly to mean adding content about diverse groups to the curriculum or expanding the canon taught in schools. It also should help students to develop more democratic racial and ethnic attitudes and to understand the cultural assumptions that underlie knowledge claims.

Another important dimension of multicultural education is equity pedagogy, in which teachers modify their teaching in ways that will facilitate the academic achievement of students from diverse racial, cultural, language and social-class groups.

WHAT RESEARCH SAYS

Educational leaders should become familiar with the research evidence about the effects of multicultural education and not be distracted by the critics of multicultural education who disregard or distort this significant body of research.

Research indicates that students come to school with many stereotypes, misconceptions and negative attitudes toward outside racial and ethnic groups. Research also indicates that the use of multicultural textbooks, other teaching materials and cooperative teaching strategies can help students to develop more positive racial attitudes and perceptions.

This research also indicates that these kinds of materials and teaching strategies can result in students choosing more friends from outside racial, ethnic and cultural groups.

Research indicates that teachers can increase the classroom participation and academic achievement of students from different ethnic groups by modifying their instruction so that it draws upon their cultural strengths. In Susan Philips' study, *The Invisible Culture: Communication in Classroom and Community on the Warm Spring Indian Reservation*, American Indian students participated more actively in class discussions when teachers used group-oriented participation structures that were consistent with their community cultures.

Researchers Kathryn Au and Roland G. Tharp, working in the Kamehameha Early Education Program in Honolulu, Hawaii, found that both student participation and standardized achievement test scores increased when they incorporated teaching strategies consistent with the cultures of Native Hawaiian students and used the children's experiences in reading instruction.

Studies summarized by Linda Darling-Hammond, a Stanford University professor and executive director of the National Center for Restructuring Education and Teaching, indicate that the academic achievement of students of color and low-income students increases when they have high-quality teachers who are experts in their content specialization, pedagogy and child development. She points to a significant study by Robert Dreeben, the University of Chicago sociologist. He found that when African-American students received high-quality instruction their reading achievement was as high as that of white students. The quality of instruction, not the race of the students, was the significant variable.

THE ROOTS OF MULTICULTURAL EDUCATION

Multicultural education grew out of the ferment of the civil rights movement of the 1960s. During this decade, African Americans embarked on a quest for their rights that was unprecedented in the United States. A major goal of the civil rights movement of the 1960s was to eliminate discrimination in public accommodations, housing, employment, and education. The consequences of the civil rights movement had a significant influence on educational institutions as ethnic groups—first African Americans and then other groups—demanded that the schools and other educational institutions reform their curricula so that they would reflect their experiences, histories, cultures, and perspectives.

James A. Banks, *Multicultural Education: Issues and Perspectives*, 1997.

School leaders should recognize that the goals of multicultural education are highly consistent with those of the nation's schools: to develop thoughtful citizens who can function effectively in the world of work and in the civic community. Ways must be found for schools to recognize and respect the cultures and languages of students from diverse groups while at the same time working to develop an overarching national culture to which all groups will have allegiance.

This can best be done by bringing groups that are on the margins of society into the center, educating students who have the knowledge, skills and values needed to rethink and change the center so that it is more inclusive and incorporating the research and theory in multicultural education into school reform.

Rethinking and re-imaging our nation in ways that will make it more just and equitable will enrich us all because the fates of all groups are tightly interconnected. Martin Luther King Jr. said, "We will live together as brothers and sisters or die separate and apart as strangers."

II

Jazz, rhythm-and-blues, gyrating dance steps, and fast-break basketball practically define American style in the eyes of the world—and all originated in African-American culture. So did several words in American English. This semester I assigned something new in the class I teach each fall in this field. Each student was responsible for a class presentation that traced a certain African or African-American style through American culture.

One student talked about how Muhammad Ali had changed boxing and the public style of athletes; he showed us a picture of himself as a baby on Ali's lap.

Another reported on white basketball great Pete Maravich and how his father, a basketball coach, taught him from an early age to copy the black athletes.

"They are the future of the game," Pres Maravich told his son, and the fancy ball-handling of Pistol Pete proved him right.

Other students reported on legislator Barbara Jordan, writers Maya Angelou and Langston Hughes, cooking, New Age medicine, and military cadence calls, originally called "Duckworths" after Private Duckworth, an African American, who introduced them to the Army.

BROADENING PERSPECTIVES

Midway through the term, a criminal justice major in his mid-30s stood up and stunned us by saying:

"I'm not going to report on something outside this class. I'm going to report on this class."

It was not what I anticipated from this student, who had not said much so far, and whose attitude I had pegged somewhere between indifferent and hostile. His report told why he felt the course ought to be required of all university students and possibly all Americans.

"I figure if there was this much I didn't know about (my own) African-American culture," he said, "I must be even more ignorant about other people. I'd like to take a course on Mexican-American culture or Native-American culture. The way I see it, they're part of what it means to be American, too."

In five minutes, this student resolved what historians and politicians on both sides of the political fence have been struggling with for the past 20 years. A course in African-American culture broadened his perspective, encouraged him to look at other Americans with greater curiosity and respect, and stimulated him to learn more about our complex and wonderfully varied cultural history.

MULTICULTURAL STUDIES ARE NOT DIVISIVE

About 35 percent of the students at my university are Mexican American and, historically in the community, relations between Mexican Americans and the much smaller minority of African Americans have not been cordial. Some Mexican Americans resent African Americans for dominating the national civil rights movement, and African Americans resent Mexican Americans for resenting them. Yet here was a black student saying he wished he knew more about Mexican Americans, and he might just take a course on the topic.

I offer his story as a response to those who believe multicultural or minority studies are splintering our national culture.

We live in a multicultural society, and our national heritage is Latino American, African American, Asian American, Jewish American, Euro-American. We are all, as writers Ralph Ellison and Albert Murray have told us for years, cultural mulattoes. Studying any one part of us does not divide us; it educates us. Occasionally, it inspires us.

> "Multiculturalism is not—and never can be—a viable educational principle."

MULTICULTURAL EDUCATION IS COUNTERPRODUCTIVE

Thomas J. Famularo

Multicultural education does not benefit students, argues Thomas J. Famularo in the following viewpoint. Multiculturalism is harmful because it attempts to deny the existence of a common American culture and emphasizes divisive group differences based on race, gender, and social class, the author contends. Moreover, Famularo maintains, multicultural curricula are often shallow and superficial, offering broad overviews of diverse subject matter rather than in-depth investigations of significant material. The use of such curricula results in a decline in educational quality, he concludes. Famularo, a former English instructor for the City University of New York, is operations manager at Bowne Financial Printers in Secaucus, New Jersey.

As you read, consider the following questions:

1. According to Peter W. Cookson, cited by Famularo, what is multiculturalism's definition of community?
2. In Famularo's opinion, what are the two "fatal flaws" of multicultural education?
3. What specific information was deleted in a history curriculum proposed by the National Education Standards and Improvement Council, according to the author?

Excerpted from Thomas J. Famularo, "The Intellectual Bankruptcy of Multiculturalism," *USA Today* magazine, May 1996. Reprinted by permission of the Society for the Advancement of Education.

It is along ideological lines that the debate over multicultural-ism has assumed its current form and substance. Thomas Sowell, in *Inside American Education*, states that the "ideological components of multiculturalism can be summarized as a cul-tural relativism which finds the prominence of Western civiliza-tion in the world or in the schools intolerable." Recently, this anti-West aspect of multiculturalism was evidenced at Yale Uni-versity, where a $20,000,000 grant by Texas billionaire Lee M. Bass, exclusively for the development of programs and courses in Western culture, met highly politicized faculty opposition, with the result that Yale returned the money.

John O'Sullivan, editor of *National Review*, decries the multicul-turalist assertion that America is an "idea rather than a nation [possessing] a distinctive but encompassing American identity." Peter W. Cookson, Jr., author of *School Choice: The Struggle for the Soul of American Education*, offers the insight that multiculturalism's hos-tility to the West and repudiation of an identifiable American culture is augmented by a radically new definition of commu-nity, one that swerves from the traditional emphasis on "family, neighborhood, church, lodge, and school to race, gender, occu-pation, and sexual preference."

These ideological divisions within U.S. society threaten to rend the nation into hostile factions. For example, Richard Bern-stein, in *Dictatorship of Virtue: Multiculturalism and the Battle for America's Future*, brands ideological multiculturalists as "radical-left inhabi-tants of a political dreamland." Its critics maintain that multicul-turalism is not—and never can be—a viable educational princi-ple.

THE EVOLUTION OF MULTICULTURALISM

A few points of clarification regarding multiculturalism's recent evolution might be helpful. What began during the early part of the twentieth century as a shift towards increased awareness of ethnic and minority contributions to American history has evolved into a pedagogy that makes diversity and difference the prime movers of the curriculum.

In response to the New York State Department of Education's *A Curriculum of Inclusion*, Diane Ravitch, writing in *The American Scholar* (Summer 1990), argued that current manifestations of multicul-turalism extend far beyond the kind of pluralism that "seeks a richer common culture" to "multicultural particularism," which denies that a "common culture is possible or desirable."

According to the authors of *A Curriculum of Inclusion*, including controversial City University of New York (CUNY) former Black

Studies chairman Leonard Jeffries, multiculturalism no longer should be construed to mean "adding marginal examples of 'other' cultures to an assumed dominant culture." On the contrary, multiculturalists adamantly gainsay the idea of an identifiable and definable American culture that might form the basis of a core curriculum. "The old curriculum is essentially based on the premise that America has one cultural heritage augmented by minor contributions from other peoples who by and large have presented 'problems' to the primary culture. To combat teaching and learning based on this premise, a radical, new approach to building a curriculum is needed," *A Curriculum of Inclusion* claims. Multicultural particularism, counters Ravitch, "is a bad idea whose time has come. It is also a fashion spreading like wildfire through the education system."

THE FLAWS OF MULTICULTURAL EDUCATION

As multiculturalism is infused into mainstream American public education, I am reminded of a question asked by a former Brooklyn College colleague which captures the ultimate unfeasibility of multicultural education: "What comes out?" Although learning should be lifelong, schooling is a finite process. Inevitably, additions to the curriculum made in the name of diversity and inclusion render the necessity of displacement. A curriculum can contain just so much, and because education succeeds only when it includes prolonged and in-depth consideration of specific books, authors, ideas, and historical events, more in education often is less.

As far back as 1984, the Committee of Correspondence, a St. Louis–based international network of educational reformers, offered both a definition and defense of multicultural education: Knowledge of "diverse intellectual and cultural traditions," they wrote, should be a primary objective of a democratic curriculum, and this knowledge must include "not only the familiar academic disciplines and traditions of high culture, but the great multiplicity of cultures, perspectives and ways of knowing of the western and non-western world."

The committee faltered, however, in regard to the possible implementation of multicultural education by allowing that "There are difficult dilemmas in how to realize [this] in everyday schools and curriculum practice." These dilemmas must be "negotiated out of the conflicting values and interests of the students, teachers, and members of the local community." The key question, which the committee did not entertain, is whether or not this process of negotiation can result in anything other than what one educator has described as "dens of babble."

Multicultural education is undermined by two fatal flaws. The first is that the more the curriculum represents a multicultural test based upon "exposure to diversity," the more shallow and superficial learning becomes. By disavowing the "difficult dilemma" of choosing what comes out, multiculturalism ultimately reduces education to its shallowest possibilities—the mere glossing over of diverse subject matter—and renders the kind of understanding that comes from intensive, prolonged study of selected material impossible to attain.

THE DANGERS OF MULTICULTURALISM

The re-racialization of American society that is taking place in the name of multiculturalism is not a progressive movement, but a step backward to the America that existed before *Brown v. Board of Education* and the passage of the major civil rights laws of the 1960s. We are at a critical juncture in our history. Even if we are not, as the multiculturalists claim, about to become a majority minority nation, racial and ethnic diversity in our population is increasing. If we allow race and ethnicity to determine public policy, we invite the kind of cleavages that will pit one group against another in ways that can not be good for the groups themselves or the society we all must live in.

Linda Chavez, *USA Today* magazine, May 1996.

Multiculturalism's second fatal flaw is that it necessarily precludes the single most important requirement for successful education—coherent means to a discernible end. By denying the existence or desirability of a distinctive American culture, thereby repudiating the need for public education to assist in the process of assimilation, multicultural education is both aimless and rudderless. Multicultural curricula careen to and fro, touching fleetingly upon cultural tidbits of theoretically limitlessly diverse groups.

A PLAGUE OF IGNORANCE

The culture wars that have ravaged American society for more than 30 years have forced America's public schools to capitulate to the relativism inherent in multiculturalism and to abandon education based upon desired ends for the cafeteria-style taste-test type of learning which does not work. Ravitch reasons that the final results of this "fractionation" are high school graduates who can "no longer be said to share a common body of knowledge, not to mention a common culture."

In an attempt to validate multiculturalism's emphasis on particularism and its concomitant subversion of cultural commonality, knowledge and facts in multicultural education consistently are subordinated to so-called "critical thinking skills." I say "so-called" because my experience with hundreds of college freshmen invariably revealed young adults who were as oblivious to real critical thinking concepts such as induction, deduction, syllogism, appeal to authority, point-counterpoint, comparison, and contrast as they were to rudimentary historical facts and dates. The dismal truth is that, more often than not, critical thinking in the classroom means little more than subjective questioning and unsubstantiated, unreasoned, personal opinion. Attempts to structure student opinion according to classical logical models often are met by multiculturalist accusations of Eurocentricity and pro-Western prejudices.

As an instructor of English at Brooklyn and Lehman Colleges of CUNY during the 1980s, I never had to look far for the results of education that substitutes critical thinking skills for the teaching of selected factual knowledge. The defining characteristic of my freshman students transcended race, sex, and ethnic heritage. Although predominantly intelligent, they essentially were empty vessels devoid of quantifiable academic information.

Contrary to the assertions of proponents of multiculturalism that limitless pluralism enriches education, the de-emphasizing of specific core material and factual knowledge in high school resulted in what it inevitably must have—a plague of ignorance. Multiculturalism's subordination of facts and knowledge to critical thinking skills demonstrates its educational bankruptcy, for any critical opinion worthy of a passing grade must evolve out of knowledge and be grounded in objective facts.

A Radical Agenda

Anyone familiar with the nation's campus culture clashes knows what the call for diversity in education too often really is—a red herring for a radical agenda. When Stanford University, for instance, recommends only three subjects of study in the music segment of its required Culture, Ideas, Values course—Reggae lyrics, Rastafarian poetry, and Andean music—it answers the question "What comes out?" with a list that includes Bach, Mozart, and Beethoven. It constructs, as well, a curriculum which, far from being representatively diverse, is unified around a theme of race and sex and the debunking of Western culture.

Ironically, many multiculturalists, either consciously or instinctively, recognize the intellectual bankruptcy of the cultural particularism they ostensibly espouse. Multicultural curricula, overtly committed to diversity and difference, almost invariably are focused on underlying, latent, and often dogmatic themes.

In what direction is multiculturalism headed? Although educators such as Thomas Sowell have written of "the multiple evidences of declining educational quality during the period when multiculturalism and other non-academic preoccupations have taken up more and more of the curriculum," educational leaders attempted to plunge ahead into the multicultural morass with the ill-conceived National Standards for United States History, a part of the Clinton Administration's Goals 2000 Act.

As is inevitable with a multicultural curriculum, in order to make room for diverse additions, the National Education Standards and Improvement Council needed to make equivalent quantitative subtractions. Omitted from this proposed curriculum—in the name of respect for diversity—were, among other touchstones of traditional American history, the First Continental Congress, Robert E. Lee, Alexander Graham Bell, Thomas Edison, Albert Einstein, Jonas Salk, and the Wright brothers. Ultimately, students educated within the vague parameters of this multicultural curriculum will learn the hard truth—that any "critical" opinion of the birth of our nation without knowledge of the First Continental Congress or of the Civil War without considering Robert E. Lee is not based on sufficient factual knowledge and, therefore, has little or no value in the marketplace of ideas. . . .

Multiculturalism, writes *National Review*'s O'Sullivan, is "liberalism deconstructing itself." He very well may be right. It will not be until the educational bankruptcy of multiculturalism is exposed fully that the deconstruction of American public education will be halted successfully.

"[The] marginalization and suppression of minority cultural identities . . . [is revealed in] the absence of minority history in school texts."

CURRICULA AND TEXTBOOKS SHOULD REFLECT MULTICULTURALISM

Cameron McCarthy

In the following viewpoint, Cameron McCarthy argues that minority histories and cultural diversity should be essential elements in school texts and curricula. Today's commonly used textbooks generally neglect alternative minority and female perspectives and offer superficial coverage of complex historical events, McCarthy contends. If teachers are to provide a comprehensive, liberating, and egalitarian education, coursework and school texts must be informed by multiculturalism, the author concludes. McCarthy is the author of *The Uses of Culture*, from which this viewpoint is excerpted.

As you read, consider the following questions:

1. What prompted the rise of multicultural education, according to McCarthy?
2. In McCarthy's view, what are the limitations of textbooks that offer "compensatory" and "contribution" histories?
3. How does the presentation of slavery in the history textbook *America: Past and Present* avoid complexity, in the author's opinion?

While developments have taken place in contemporary popular culture toward a certain radical eclecticism—a postmodern sensibility in the areas of art, architecture, music, and literature, that in some ways brazenly absorbs third world and ethnic images—the school system, particularly the school curriculum, remains steadfastly monological. For example, while popular artists such as David Byrne and Paul Simon directly incorporate Afro-Brazilian and South African styles into their music (albums such as *Rei Momo* and *Grace Land* are good examples), and while minority artists like Spike Lee, Julie Dash, and the Afro-Asian Black Arts movement in England have begun to influence new ethnic themes in television and film culture, American educators have responded with a decided lack of enthusiasm for cultural diversity and, at times, with a sense of moral panic with respect to the demands for a ventilation of the school curriculum. It is this administrative hostility to diversity that, over the years, has propelled minority agitation for multiculturalism in schooling.

Driven forward by demands from racially subordinated groups for fundamental reforms in race relations in education and society, and by the efforts of mainstream educators to provide practical solutions to the problem of racial inequality in the United States, multicultural education emerged in the late 1960s as a powerful challenge to the Eurocentric foundations of the American school curriculum. Multiculturalism is a product of a particular historical conjuncture of relations among the state, contending racial minority/majority groups, educators, and policy intellectuals in the United States when the discourse over schools became increasingly racialized. From the first, African-Americans and other minority groups emphasized a variety of transformative themes, insisting that curriculum and education policy address the vital questions of the distribution of power and representation in schools and the status of minority cultural identities in curriculum organization and arrangements. . . .

Within the last two decades, the transformative themes of the multicultural movement have been steadily "sucked back into the system." As departments of education, textbook publishers, and intellectual entrepreneurs pushed more normative themes of cultural understanding and sensitivity training, the actual implementation of an emancipatory multiculturalism in the school curriculum and in pedagogical and teacher education practices in the university has been effectively deferred. (Emancipatory multiculturalism is defined here as the critical redefinition of school knowledge from the heterogeneous perspectives and identities of racially disadvantaged groups—a process that goes beyond the language of "inclusivity" and emphasizes relationality and multivocality as the central intellectual forces in the production of knowledge.) . . .

WESTERNNESS AND THE AMERICAN IDENTITY

Educators and textbook publishers have directly participated in the trotting out of a particularly cruel fantasy about the story of civilization and this society—one in which the only knowledge worth knowing and the only stories worth telling are associated with the handiworks of the bards of Greece and Rome. Within this frame of reference, art, architecture, music, and science, and democracy are portrayed as the fertile products of Europeans and their caucasian counterparts in the United States. It is, as Caribbean poet and political activist Aime Cesaire would say, "a funny little tale to tell." This is, in fact, the essence of taught knowledge. Through the school curriculum and its centerpiece, the textbook, American schoolchildren come to know the world as one made by European ancestors and white people generally. The world that schoolchildren come to know is, on the other hand, a world overpopulated by minorities and third world people, a world, according to Allan Bloom, "brought to ruination," by these peoples of other lands. Contemporary conservative writers have sought to reinvigorate these myths. Bloom maintains in *The Closing of the American Mind* that it was the protests of African-American students and women in the 1960s that brought this country's university system and its curriculum to the present nadir. The reason why we are doing so poorly compared to the Japanese, others maintain, can be explained by the fact that we let the underprepared masses into the schools and the universities in the '60s. Others, such as Diane Ravitch, contend that though the American populace is diverse, the primary cultural and institutional coherence that currently exists in our society is unequivocally European in origin. It is the durability of these European values of order, democracy, and tolerance, Ravitch maintains, that has protected "us" from the cultural chaos afflicting countries in Eastern Europe, the Middle East, Africa, and Asia. (In a 1990 essay published in the journal *American Educator*, Ravitch writes "The political and economic institutions of the United States were deeply influenced by European ideas. Europe's legacy to us is the set of moral and political values that we Americans subsequently refined and reshaped to enable us, in all our diversity, to live together in freedom and peace.")

But these kinds of remonstrations get us nowhere beyond nostalgia and its obverse, cynicism. Here we can find no real solace—no new ideas to help guide us through the events and challenges of the present era. This rather philistine reassertion of Eurocentrism and Westernness is itself a wish to run away from the task of coming to terms with the fundamental historical currents that have shaped this country—an impulse to deny the fundamentally, "plural," immigrant, and Afro–New World character that defines historical and current relations among minority/majority groups in the United States. . . .

THE TEXTBOOK

Nowhere is this marginalization and suppression of minority cultural identities more in evidence than in the textbook industry in terms of the absence of minority history in school texts, and in terms of the exclusion of emancipatory indigenous scholarship in the process of textbook production altogether. But as I will argue, changes in the contents of textbooks are only one aspect of what is necessary for meaningful reform toward the goal of a genuine multicultural curriculum and school experiences for all students. There is, in fact, a need to look at a range of elements in the institutional culture of schools, the constraints and barriers to teacher ingenuity, and the educational priorities set in district offices, by building principals, and in teacher education programs in our universities. In all of these areas, emancipatory multiculturalism, as a form of what cultural critics Henry Giroux and George Wood call critical literacy, is now suppressed.

THE COMPLEXITY OF AMERICAN IDEALS

Nothing could be more central to our "national ideals" than freedom. Surely, here is a common theme of American history and a cause for celebration. Yet freedom—like other national ideals—is not a fixed set of ideas inherited from England and institutionalized by the founding fathers. It is a persistent source of conflict, whose definition has changed over time and whose meaning has been profoundly affected by the struggles of "groups who have felt themselves far off American history's main track" to gain their full rights. The meaning of American freedom has been constructed not only in congressional debates and political treatises, but also on plantations and picket lines, in parlors and bedrooms. Frederick Douglass, Eugene V. Debs, and Margaret Sanger—the kind of individuals whose highlighting in the 1994 National History Standards so alarmed critics—are its architects as well as Thomas Jefferson and Abraham Lincoln.

Eric Foner, *American Scholar*, Winter 1998.

---

evidence of their struggle for freedom. As early as 1657 Africans and Indians in Hartford "joined in an uprising and destroyed some buildings" in the settlement. Such incidents were regularly repeated.

In sharp contrast to the works of Harding and James, the bland, non-conflictual writing that one finds in many textbooks is in part a product of the highly routine, unchanging approach to textbook production conducted in the textbook industry. As publishers work to maximize markets and profits, textbook writing has become increasingly more and more like an assembly-line process in which multiple authors produce submissions that are checked for quality control, readability, and overly controversial content issues by keen editorial staffs. When the textbook finally becomes a finished product, we have a tool for teaching that is often uninteresting and unchallenging to students and teachers alike. By bargaining away issues that might offend state adoption committees and conservative interest groups, publishers, and textbook writers contribute to the marginalization of cultural diversity and the suppression of minority history and identities in textbooks.

MULTICULTURAL REFORM

As indicated previously in this viewpoint, we must see the textbook as only one aspect of a broad set of practices that impact on the institutional environment of the school. . . .

For the multicultural curriculum to be fully realized in schools, the following specific initiatives are absolutely critical:

• Preservice teacher education programs at the universities and colleges across the country must systematically incorporate critical multicultural objectives into their curricula and field experiences.

• School districts and school principals must set diversity as an explicit goal and seek ways to integrate the notion in the organization of the curriculum and the institutional life of schools. Right now, multiculturalism is treated as a side topic, mentioned only during Black History Month and on International Women's Day.

• Multiculturalism should not be limited to the present understanding—that is, the idea that all we need to do is to add some content about minorities and women to the school curriculum. Multiculturalism must involve a radical rethinking of the nature of school knowledge as knowledge that is fundamentally relational and heterogeneous in character. In this sense, for example, we cannot get a full understanding of the civil rights movement in the United States without studying its multiplier

Let us now consider the relationship of the textbook and the textbook industry to multicultural education. It is important to recognize from the outset that textbooks embody real, lived relations of representation, production, and consumption that tend more or less to suppress minority identities and reproduce existing social inequalities. By "representation," I am not simply referring to the presence or absence of pictures of minorities in textbooks. By representation, I mean the whole process of who gets to define whom, when, and how. Who has control over the production of pictures and images in this society? I believe that textbook production is an important dimension of a much broader social and political context in which minorities, women, and the physically and mentally disabled have little control over the process of the production of images about themselves. I mean, for example, that when incidents like the Los Angeles Police Department's beating of Rodney King occurs, black people do not have equal access to the media to tell their side of the story. So is it true in the case of textbooks.

In an essay entitled "Placing Women in History: Definitions and Challenges," the feminist historian Gerder Lerner maintains that the treatment of women in contemporary textbooks can be described as presenting "compensatory" or "contribution" histories of the experiences of women in the United States. By compensatory history, Lerner refers to the tendency of dominant history textbooks to identify and single out what she calls "women worthies." This kind of history of notable women celebrates the achievements of individual women such as Jane Adams, Elizabeth Cady Stanton, Harriet Tubman, and so on, but compensatory history of this kind tends to marginalize the agency of the broad masses of minority and working-class women. As such, these compensatory textbooks, while more inclusive than earlier books, are not exemplars of emancipatory or transformative scholarship.

THE TREATMENT OF MINORITIES IN TEXTBOOKS

This notion of compensatory history also applies to the treatment of minorities in textbooks. In the case of history, social studies, literature, and other discipline-based textbooks, minorities are added into an existing "order of things." One half of a page here and one half of a page there discusses slavery, Harriet Tubman, or "The Peaceful Warrior," Martin Luther King, Jr. There is no systematic reworking or restructuring of school knowledge, no attempt to present history from an alternative minority perspective. This fragmentary approach is also demonstrated in the treatment of the third world peoples of Africa, Latin America, and Asia. For instance, the editors of *Interracial Books for Children Bulletin*, in an in-depth review of a "representative sample" of seventy-one social studies textbooks used in the '80s in American schools, report the following:

> Central America is entirely omitted from many of the most common world geography, history, and "cultures" textbooks used in U.S. classrooms. Thirty-one U.S. history texts were checked for their coverage of Central America. Seven of these do not even mention Central America. Fifteen texts limit coverage of Central America to the building of the Panama Canal, and most of these books ignore or mention only in passing the U.S. military intervention that led to the acquisition of the canal. . . . Not one of the thirty-one texts discusses the continuing involvement of the U.S. government—sometimes overt, sometimes covert—in Central America.

The U.S. imperial presence in Latin America is often narrated in a highly mythological discourse in which the United States emerges as the good Samaritan. The natives of South America cannot do without "our" help. U.S. paternalism is not only what the Latin Americans want, it is what is needed "down there" to keep hostile foreign powers from swallowing up the region and threatening "us":

> For a long time, the United States has been interested in Latin America. First, we have a large trade with our Latin-American neighbors. They send us products that we need and enjoy, such as tin, copper, coffee, bananas and chocolate. In turn, their people buy many products from the United States. Second, the United States has tried to keep the Americas free from foreign control. If a strong and unfriendly nation controlled the nations near us, it would be a threat to the safety of the United States. (M. Schwartz and J. Connor, *Exploring American History*)

This highly ethnocentric approach to history and social studies textbooks is stabilized by a language of universality and objectivity. In this way, the textbook is a central site for the preservation of a selective tradition in the school curriculum—one that pushes minorities and third world peoples to the outside, to the edge, to the point of deviance.

AVOIDING COMPLEXITY

Perhaps the most pernicious feature of this dominant approach to school knowledge and textbook preparation is the tendency to avoid complexity and conflict. For example, in D. King and C. Anderson's *America: Past and Present*, a fifth-grade social studies text

used in Wisconsin's elementary schools, the only s cussion of the experiences of African Americans is i of slavery. Here, the treatment of slavery as a topic perfunctory manner, and the relations between blacks on the slave plantation is described in benig of the symbolic and physical violence that chara slaves' daily existence. Complete with supporting ill life on the plantation that make the slave plantatio California vineyard with the slaves living comf snugly in their cabins, *America: Past and Present* describe plantation in the following terms:

> On any plantation you visited in the South you woul all of the farm workers were black slaves. Southern p came to depend on slavery. By 1750 there were more s free people in South Carolina. On the plantation you slaves live in cabins near the fields. Since the slaves get for their work, they depend on their owners for clo food. The food is mostly salt pork and corn. Some of have tiny plots of land where they can grow vegetables.

It is interesting to compare this description with t on the slave plantation of indigenous authors such Harding in his, *There Is a River*, or C.L.R. James in *The B* In his discussion of slavery in Haiti, James draws on t ness account:

> A Swiss traveller has left a famous description of a gang at work. "They were about a hundred men and women (ent ages, all occupied in digging ditches in a cane-field, jority of them naked or covered with rags. The sun shor with full force on their heads. . . . A mournful silence Exhaustion was stamped on every face, but the hour of not yet come. The pitiless eye of the Manager patrolled t and several foremen armed with long whips moved peri between them, giving stinging blows to all who, worn fatigue, were compelled to take a rest—men or women or old." This was no isolated picture. The sugar plantati manded an exacting and ceaseless labour.

In *There Is a River*, Harding draws attention to anothe sion of plantation life given short shrift in history t used in our schools: the topic of black liberation stru makes the following contention about the impact of l struggles on the planter-mercantile class in colonial Ame

> But it was not in Virginia and South Carolina alone, no among white Southern society, that the fear of a black qu freedom existed; the same attitude permeated much of No: colonial life. In the Northern colonies blacks had already

effects on the expansion of democratic practices to excluded groups in Australia, the Caribbean, Africa, England, and the United States itself. Further, we cannot properly understand the development of European societies without an understanding of the direct link between Europe's development and the under-development of the third world. For example, at the time that the French were helping to bankroll the American Revolution, two-thirds of France's export earnings were coming from its exploitation of sugar cane plantations in Haiti.

• Such a reworking of school knowledge must go a step further toward a reconsideration of the privileging of Eurocentric perspectives and points of view in the curriculum as reflected in, for example, the "famous men" approach to history. The "new" multicultural curriculum must go beyond the "language of inclusion" toward a "language of critique." This would involve the affirmation of minority identities and perspectives as the organizing principles for school knowledge. In this manner, schools would be sites for multicultural curriculum reform and pedagogical practices that are truly liberatory. . . .

• In terms of textbooks, there is a need to involve indigenous minority and third world scholars and teachers in the production of school knowledge in the textbook industry at every level—that is, from the level of textbook writing, through editorial and managerial decision making.

• Lastly, . . . *the multicultural ethos in schools will only be fully realized when minority and underprivileged students have access to an academic core curriculum that is on par with their middle-class and white counterparts.*

"Multiculturalists . . . frequently damn the facts in promoting their ideology."

TEXTBOOKS FAVORING MULTICULTURALISM DISTORT HISTORY

Alvin J. Schmidt

Supporters of multicultural education often argue that school curricula and texts should be revised so that they include more female and minority perspectives. In the following viewpoint, Alvin J. Schmidt contends that textbooks promoting multiculturalism actually distort history. Such texts, he maintains, often emphasize relatively insignificant accounts about minorities and women and unfairly malign Euro-American culture. In a misguided attempt to enhance minority self-esteem, Schmidt reports, multiculturalists' textbooks ignore the negative events in minority histories and omit the positive achievements of Western civilization. Schmidt is the author of *The Menace of Multiculturalism: Trojan Horse in America*, from which this viewpoint is taken.

As you read, consider the following questions:

1. In Schmidt's view, in what way do multiculturalists' books resemble Plato's definition of "noble lies?"
2. According to the author, what facts about slavery do multiculturalists' textbooks typically omit?
3. By what standard do multiculturalists judge historical figures, in Schmidt's opinion?

Excerpted from *The Menace of Multiculturalism*, by Alvin J. Schmidt. Copyright ©1997 by Alvin J. Schmidt. Reproduced with permission of Greenwood Publishing Group, Inc., Westport, Conn.

The nineteenth-century German philosopher, Georg Friedrich Hegel, responding to a student's interjection "But sir, what you say does not agree with the facts," replied: "Let the facts be damned." Undoubtedly, Hegel made this remark because he wanted his views to prevail. He might even have had good reasons for wanting to ignore or damn the facts. This might also be true of some multiculturalists, who frequently damn the facts in promoting their ideology.

Historical omissions and distortions abound in multiculturalists' publications. The negative or harmful practices of non-Western or minority cultures are typically omitted, and in the rare instances when they are noted, they are presented in an innocuous manner. On the other hand, the Euro-American's cultural shortcomings, or negative cultural practices, are cited wherever possible and are often portrayed at great length. The great achievements of the Western world are portrayed as being no more important than the far less spectacular accomplishments of non-Western societies. Sometimes even new "facts" are created, for example, the multiculturalists claim that Crispus Attucks, killed in the Boston Massacre in 1770, was black; that Western civilization was stolen from Africa; that the American Indians were highly conscientious ecologically; that the Constitution of the United States was shaped by the Iroquois Indians; and others. This tactic is reminiscent of the "noble lies" that Plato talked about in *The Republic* in which such lies were intended to persuade kings and the populace to achieve worthy objectives. Thus the multiculturalists who publish their revised histories present as significant and authentic history undocumented and highly dubious accounts about minor persons or events, usually with some ties to some minority group. The idea is to appease and please, apparently to help such groups overcome the "oppression" that has been imposed on them by the "Eurocentric" American culture.

DISCUSSIONS OF SLAVERY

True multiculturalism essentially consists of teaching students about other cultures, including the positive and negative components of given cultures. But as we have noted, the promoters of multiculturalism primarily illustrate the negative cultural practices of the Euro-American culture.

When present-day textbooks discuss slavery, they only cover slavery as it existed in America or other Western societies, and they consistently ignore the practice of slavery in non-Western cultures. For example, textbooks say nothing about the many

American Indian tribes who practiced slavery long before Columbus and other Europeans came to America. The widely used grade school text, United States and Its Neighbors, authored by James Banks et al., discusses slavery on at least twenty pages, but makes no mention of the American Indians' practice of slavery. The same is true of another widely used grade school text, The American Nation. Nor is there any reference to it in National Standards for United States History, one of the three books highly publicized as a national school guide for teaching multiculturalism.

Nontextbooks favoring multiculturalism also omit slavery in non-Western societies. One such example is Kilpatrick Sale's book The Conquest of Paradise, which contains no reference to slavery as it was practiced by numerous American Indian tribes long before the white man arrived. Nor does it make any reference to Almond W. Lauber's book Indian Slavery in Colonial Times. Lauber describes many instances of slavery among America's Indians before the Europeans arrived. For instance, in the St. Augustine area of Florida in 1565 some natives held Cuban Indians as slaves, and in 1616, the Dutch navigator, Henrickson, encountered slaveowning Indians in the Schuylkill River area of Pennsylvania. The Illinois Indians at times bartered their slaves with the Ottawa Indians and the Iroquois. The Pima of Arizona enslaved Apache and Yuma Indians. Lauber is not the only source for data on the institution of slavery among the Indians. The multivolume publication by Reuben Gold Thwaites's Early Western Travels, 1748–1846 also documents slavery among many Indian tribes. Thwaites states that the Pawnee Indians, for example, were so "frequently enslaved by their [Indian] enemies, [that] the term 'Pani' [Pawnee] became equivalent to Indian slave."

Slavery is a moral evil, and that fact does not change, regardless of what group practiced it. Textbooks provide a necessary and valuable public service by discussing the immorality of the practice, and they need to emphasize that it is evil in every society and not just in American culture. But Americans, of course, will never know anything about the past slavery habits of American Indians if such facts are omitted.

MULTICULTURALIST OMISSIONS

Lack of reference to the slavery customs of American Indians is not the only omission in multiculturalist texts. When the importation of slaves from Africa to America is described, only rarely is it mentioned that native Africans sold their own people to the Europeans. Multiculturalists especially ignore John Thornton's 1992 book (Africa and Africans) which notes the cooperation of African slave captors: "The Atlantic slave trade" Thornton claims, "grew out of and was rationalized by African societies who participated in it and had complete control over it until the slaves were loaded onto European ships for transfer to Atlantic societies."

Another omission pertains to the slavery that existed in many African countries long before the Europeans ever practiced it, as shown by David R. James. When one does find such a reference, it is mentioned only tangentially or minimized. The school text *The World Past and Present* is a case in point. This book does briefly note African slavery, but it quickly minimizes it by saying that under this system of slavery "enslaved people were not treated as harshly and could sometimes gain their freedom after working for many years. The practice of slavery changed dramatically when the Europeans became involved."

Distorting History

The new [multicultural] texts present American dealings with Indian populations not as war between incompatible cultures, but as something explained by racism. *America: Pathways to the Present* is typical. It perpetuates the myth of the noble Indian with the story of Tecumseh and his brother Tenskwatawa, who leave "a vital legacy of defiance of invasion and respect for themselves, their people, and their culture. In later years, they would be a model for Native Americans reclaiming their traditions." In this text, students learn about the massacres at Sand Creek and Wounded Knee, which point to the racism of the oppressors, but never hear of the cruel and vicious treatment of settlers at the hands of Indians in the Wyoming Massacre, the scalping of women and children at Ft. Mims, or hundreds of other brutal and horrific encounters.

David Warren Saxe, *Weekly Standard*, March 10, 1997.

Grade school textbooks also fail to mention that slavery lasted much longer in African and Asian countries than in the British empire or in the United States. For instance, Ethiopians did not outlaw slavery until 1942, India not until 1976, and Mauritania, an African country, waited until the 1980s. In March 1996, an article appeared in *Reader's Digest* showing that slavery exists even today in the African country of Sudan.

Granted, textbook space is limited, and it is impossible to include everything that is important in a given volume. But lack of space does not prevent the inclusion of negative incidents involving Western or American culture. If multiculturalist writers of texts were truly interested in teaching students about all cultures, they not only would include negative incidents of non-Western cultures, but would also note how Western and American culture eliminated unjust practices such as slavery.

Who Opposed Slavery?

Early in the life of the Christian church (about A.D. 55), St. Paul told Philemon to take back his runaway slave, Onesimus and to treat him "no longer as a slave but more than a slave, as a beloved brother" (Philemon 16). Many biblical scholars see this New Testament document by Paul as the first Christian seed that eventually grew to abolish slavery, first by the British and then by others.

St. Paul was not the only early Christian leader who opposed slavery. St. Gregory of Nyssa (fourth century) preached on the evils of slavery, as did St. Chrysostom, a contemporary of St. Gregory, often called the golden-mouthed preacher. He said that in Christ no one was a slave. Two other church fathers in the fourth century, Lactantius and St. Ambrose, voiced similar exhortations.

Unfortunately, the institutionalized church sometimes ignored St. Paul's and many of its early leaders' directives, by condoning and sometimes even supporting slavery in many countries. Throughout the church's existence, however, some Christian leaders continued to condemn slavery. One such person was St. Olaf, who in the eleventh century banned slavery in Norway. In more recent times, it was the influence of William Wilberforce, a British member of Parliament, who, moved by Christian teachings, fought to outlaw slavery. After twenty years of labor and toil, his arguments led England to ban slavery in 1833 throughout the expansive British empire. This, and similar evidence, is of no significance to multiculturalists. They ignore observations such as the following one by Suzanne Miers: "The great blossoming of Protestant and then Catholic missionary activity in the nineteenth century was intimately connected with the abolition of the slave trade." If multiculturalists were truly interested in pointing out the merits of all cultures, they would emphasize the motives and forces in Western and American culture that led to the abolition of slavery. . . .

Slighting Euro-American History

The multiculturalists' role is to make non-Western minority groups feel good about themselves, and they try to do this in two ways. One method is to slight the Euro-American culture. If members of minority cultures read about the sins and shortcomings of the Euro-Americans, they will conclude that the cultural practices of their ancestors were free of such sins, and thus they will feel good about themselves and their ancestors.

The second method is to cite some example or incident that a minority member, or his or her ancestral group, reportedly contributed to American culture. Such favorable mention will enhance the self-esteem of present members who identify with the group in question. Empirically, this is a flawed argument. Most people's self-esteem comes from doing something worthwhile themselves rather than receiving it vicariously from their ancestors. The second tack conveys a certain amount of irony because it implies that the maligned Euro-American culture perhaps is not so bad as multiculturalists would have people believe—that is, if minorities made some contribution to it.

This second method frequently ignores the facts of history to accomplish its goal. This is not surprising inasmuch as multiculturalists operate according to the Marxist principle that the end justifies the means. A few examples of teaching feel-good history follow.

FEEL-GOOD HISTORY FOR MINORITIES AND WOMEN

One study by Robert Lerner and associates found that textbook writers in the 1970s and 1980s cited individuals and historical events that involved minority characters who previously (in the 1960s) did not merit historical mention, much less extended discussion of them. In fact, they often receive more page space than individuals who made immensely greater contributions. In one textbook, for instance, Crispus Attucks (one of several Americans killed in the Boston Massacre in 1770) receives more extensive coverage than Paul Revere. Attucks, by some authors, is said to be a black man, even though his racial identity has never been positively ascertained. W.E.B. Du Bois, a black writer, is more prominently covered than Booker T. Washington, whose reputation has suffered among minorities for his conservative views. Harriet Beecher Stowe, author of Uncle Tom's Cabin, who exposed the evils of slavery to millions of Americans, is now often cited less frequently in texts than is Harriet Tubman, the black woman who helped about 300 black slaves escape by way of the "Underground Railroad." That she was assisted by white abolitionists is totally ignored.

In another article, Robert Lerner and his colleagues show that one textbook, in discussing the Civil War, provides photographs of three female nurses but none of General Grant or General Sherman. Still another account praises a 16-year-old female, Sybil Ludington, who in 1777 undertook "an urgent mission" in a "daring" ride to alert the state militia during the American Revolutionary War. She is portrayed as cold and tired, but nevertheless she continues her ride. Even though she managed to rouse the militia, the British troops still escaped. Her failure is not noted. All the same, she received two and a quarter inches of page space, while Paul Revere received only faint mention.

In the history textbook *American Odyssey*, a book of 880 pages, Paul Revere also is totally ignored, but one-half page is devoted to a picture showing Mrs. Schuyler burning a wheat field on the approach of the British soldiers. This textbook is authored by Gary Nash, one of the authors of the highly controversial and avidly pro-multiculturalist three-volume 1994 *National Standards*. These volumes also exclude Paul Revere from American history.

Excluding Paul Revere is a big loss, for he was no ordinary Patriot. Not only was his ride to Lexington highly successful, but also he successfully completed a ride to Lexington two days before the well-publicized one. In the earlier ride, he informed John Hancock and Samuel Adams about British plans to march on Concord to capture the Patriots' arsenal. This ride helped the Americans prepare for the eventful day of April 19, 1775. Seven months earlier, September 11, 1774, he left by horseback from Boston to ride to Philadelphia, where he arrived on September 17, to deliver the Suffolk Resolves to the first Continental Congress. It was a ride of 315 miles. One historian says: "He traveled thousands of miles on horseback during troublesome times." He also set up a gunpowder mill after he made a mental picture of the manufacturing process on his tour of a mill in Philadelphia. Some historians also list him as a member of the Boston Tea Party. Nonetheless, today he is either completely ignored or has been relegated to obscurity in favor of relatively minor figures. This revisionism has been motivated to please women and minority groups, as well as to minimize accounts devoted to white males who too closely reflect Western standards and values. . . .

The "White-Male Hegemony"

Those who seek to give Paul Revere and other well-established American heroes the honor they deserve and once received are said to support "white-male hegemony." In keeping with Marxist ideology, multiculturalists believe that people's race, sex, or ethnicity determines and shapes their view of reality. Multiculturalists therefore judge historical figures by this standard. The existing values and practices of Western societies are seen to be the product of white males. The longstanding Western position that ideas transcend people's race or ethnicity is also seen as a white-male construct that needs to be eliminated. Whenever complaints are voiced about the frequent distortions of history that are reflected in today's school texts, the multiculturalist response is that such criticisms are merely desperate acts of white males, intent on protecting their vested interests.

"Immigrant students of Hispanic descent who are bilingual and attend bilingual programs do much better academically than those who speak English only."

BILINGUAL EDUCATION IS BENEFICIAL

Ofelia Garcia

In June 1998, California voters passed Proposition 227, a measure that ends public bilingual education programs in that state. In the following viewpoint, Ofelia Garcia contends that the implementation of Proposition 227 will prove to be a setback for California's immigrant students. Research proves that well-planned bilingual education programs that emphasize fluency in both English and Spanish enable Hispanic immigrants to excel academically. Moreover, Garcia argues, bilingual education for all students would benefit American society by enhancing communication and understanding among different ethnicities and language groups. Garcia is dean of the School of Education at the Brooklyn campus of Long Island University. She is also co-editor of *The Multilingual Apple: Languages in New York City.*

As you read, consider the following questions:

1. When was the nation's first bilingual education act passed?
2. According to the author, why is it important for immigrant students to learn their first language well before learning a second language?
3. How do the changes in New York City's Latino immigrant population over the past thirty years illustrate the need for flexible bilingual education programs, in Garcia's opinion?

Reprinted from Ofelia Garcia, "California Vote Does English No Favors," *Newsday*, June 4, 1998, by permission of the author.

Civil Rights advocates warned that Proposition 209, California's 1996 ban on affirmative action programs, would have disastrous results for minorities, including closing public university doors at an alarming rate to black and Hispanic students with good potential.

And, based on recent data released by the University of California's premier campuses at Berkeley and Los Angeles, showing steep drops in admissions of black, Hispanic and Native American applicants for 1998's fall freshman class, the warning has proved to be well-founded.

And in June 1998, Californians again went to the polls, where one of the items they voted on—and passed 61 percent to 39 percent—Proposition 227, was a measure that can be expected to have similarly disastrous results for minorities. It will dismantle all bilingual public educational programs at all levels, regardless of effectiveness.

ERODING EDUCATIONAL INCLUSIVENESS

This will not only further erode affirmative action, but also will erode the very educational foundation of inclusiveness that has strengthened the social fabric of America, especially since 1968, when the country's first bilingual education act was passed.

In fact, what has made American education distinctively strong is its inclusiveness, through which excellence is enriched by differences.

California provides an array of programs to assist students who are learning English. All schools have English as a Second Language classes, but some use English exclusively to teach while others also have bilingual instruction in which native languages are used to teach basic subjects while students learn English.

This flexibility will be expunged by Proposition 227 and replaced with a yearlong program in which all subjects will be taught in English unless a child-by-child case has been made for special treatment. In effect, all students will be obliged to learn English in one year, even though many children require much more support for learning any language, not to mention for being able to function academically in the language.

This approach, born out of dissatisfaction among a group of Latino parents with ineffective bilingual classes at a Los Angeles elementary school and quickly adopted by opportunistic but terribly misguided politicians, has nothing to do with well-established insights into human development, human intelligence, or learning theory.

Rather, it is just another political misstep on the path to educational elitism in the guise of so-called higher national standards. The danger of adopting policies designed to standardize education lies in their inability to recognize that universal prescriptions are oblivious to the needs of children as learners and persons.

The Benefits of Bilingualism

Proposition 227 proponents argued that bilingual education programs in California are havens for poor instruction and even poorer achievement. Yet national and international research shows that bilingualism and biliteracy have beneficial psycho-cognitive results.

In fact, immigrant students of Hispanic descent who are bilingual and attend bilingual programs do much better academically than those who speak English only. Taking into account a significant number of differentials, including socio-economic status, the latter group has lower performances on standardized tests, poorer school attendance and a higher drop-out rate.

Tony Auth. ©1998 Philadelphia Inquirer. Reprinted with permission of Universal Press Syndicate. All rights reserved.

I can cite numerous studies that conclude that for children, and adults with limited schooling, the first language is an essential pedagogic tool for transmitting knowledge and information effectively. Using the first language accelerates a student's acquisition of a second language and the use of that language academically.

Just as bilingual education produces tremendous benefits for students, so too does it have a positive impact on society at large. The Yeshiva University sociolinguist Joshua Fishinan and I have shown, for example, how New York City has used its multilingualism to become the global business metropolis it is today. Leaders in the European Union and other international coalitions have embraced multilingualism as one of the most important assets for success in our increasingly complex and highly challenging global economy.

Academic Differences Among Immigrants

Proponents of Proposition 227 would rather go in a different direction than the rest of the world. They want to confine all students with language differences to an all-encompassing educational straitjacket, without regard to the academic differences of today's wave of immigrants.

For example, in New York City, Latino immigration has changed in the last 30 years.

Previously, the majority of immigrants were Puerto Rican, coming from a school system deeply influenced by that of the United States. Now, more and more immigrants are from Latin American countries with poorer educational traditions. Many of these students arrive with limited schooling and limited literacy in their native language and confront educational demands not present decades ago. They do not have sufficient first-language skills or the content knowledge necessary to develop a second language quickly and to comprehend instruction. First and foremost, they must become readers and writers; how can they do so if not taught in a language they already understand?

Proposition 227 advocates also need to understand that bilingual education is more than a language program. For a majority of schoolchildren, bilingualism and biliteracy can bring about greater understanding among ethnicities and increased knowledge of each other. In fact, bilingual education can combat inequality between different language groups.

What, then, does it say of a society that has propagated and promoted equal opportunity for its citizenry when there is a move—in the form of Proposition 227—that could lead to a complete cutoff of a significant segment of its population?

Are we a nation in denial of our demographics?

"The best policy . . . for the country is to teach English to immigrant and nonimmigrant children as quickly as possible."

BILINGUAL EDUCATION IS A FAILURE

Linda Chavez

Bilingual education programs are largely a failure, argues Linda Chavez in the following viewpoint. These programs—which typically offer years of instruction solely in an immigrant student's native language—usually do not increase students' language skills, Chavez contends. There is no evidence that proves that immigrants must become fluent in their first language before learning English, she reports. In fact, students who are placed in bilingual programs often end up illiterate in both their native language and English. Policymakers should end bilingual education and promote instruction in English for language-minority children, she concludes. Chavez is the president of the Center for Equal Opportunity in Washington, D.C., and the author of *Out of the Barrio: Toward a New Politics of Hispanic Assimilation*.

As you read, consider the following questions:

1. According to Chavez, what was the goal of the first bilingual education program?
2. What were the results of Christine Rossell's review of three hundred bilingual-education studies?
3. According to the author, how do the majority of immigrants feel about bilingual education?

A mother should know.

To measure the success of bilingual education in America, listen to the testimonies of some Hispanic mothers who are suing the state of New York for keeping their children in bilingual programs beyond the state-mandated three years. Juana Zarzuela testified that her son was transferred from bilingual education to special education despite her objection to his participation in either program. "My son has been in bilingual education for five years and in special education since 1994. [He] cannot read or write in English or Spanish," she said. Carmen Quinones testified, "My son is in ninth grade and has been in bilingual education since he entered the school system. My son is confused between Spanish and English."

Ada Jimenez testified that her grandson also cannot read or write in either language after five years of bilingual education. According to Jimenez: "I personally met one of his teachers in the bilingual program who did not speak any English. We were told that because my grandson has a Spanish last name, he should remain in bilingual classes." Because of his name, the school put Jimenez's grandson into a bilingual program in which up to 80 percent of his day was spent in Spanish—even though he did not speak any Spanish.

Parents aren't the only ones upset about bilingual education. Edwin Selzer, an assistant principal for social studies at one New York high school, testified that "once a child was in a bilingual program, he remained in such a program and was never mainstreamed into English-speaking classes. Even when students themselves asked to withdraw from the bilingual program, the assistant principal [for] foreign languages did not grant their request." Selzer also stated that "even the Spanish skills of students in bilingual programs were poor—many students graduating from Eastern District High School were illiterate in both English and Spanish." . . .

THE HISTORY OF BILINGUAL EDUCATION

Bilingual education began in the late sixties as a small, $7.5 million federal program primarily for Mexican-American children. The idea was to teach them in Spanish for a short period until they got up to speed in English. Democratic Sen. Ralph Yarborough of Texas, a leading sponsor of the first federal bilingual law in 1968, explained that its intent was "to make children fully literate in English" and "not to make the mother tongue dominant." Unfortunately, bilingual education soon fell under the sway of political activists who promoted native-language instruction as a civil right. In fact, the Supreme Court's *Lau vs. Nichols* decision in 1974 held that the civil rights of language-minority children were being violated unless they were offered some program to ensure they receive an equal educational opportunity. The court did not, however, require native-language instruction. The U.S. Commission on Civil Rights, nevertheless, used *Lau* as an excuse to insist that schools offer bilingual education or face a cutoff of federal funds.

The reason bilingual education is failing so many of America's students is because it relies on a flawed theory. This theory states that to become fully proficient in a new language, a student first must be literate and proficient in his or her native language. This means that non-English-proficient children must be taught to read and write in their native language in a five- to seven-year program in which up to 80 percent of their day is spent hearing, speaking, reading and writing their native language. Unfortunately almost no empirical evidence supports this theory, which ignores virtually everything we know about language acquisition. The theory itself was not developed until after bilingual education was institutionalized around the United States and is more a rationalization than a legitimate educational theory.

FLAWED RESEARCH

Several published studies prove that the push for bilingual education is based more upon political muscle-flexing by the ethnic and education lobbies than upon sound educational theory. The best that can be said in favor of bilingual education is that its efficacy is unproved. In fact, most research that would seem to validate bilingual education is unsound. The Congressional Research Service conducted a review of bilingual education and found that, at best, the evidence was inconclusive. Even Professor Kenji Hakuta, a leading advocate of bilingual education, admitted in 1986 that "an awkward tension blankets the lack of empirical demonstration of the success of bilingual-education programs." The National Academy of Sciences, or NAS, reviewed two Department of Education studies of bilingual education in 1992 and found them so methodologically unsound as to be useless. These two major studies were so bad that the NAS actually recommended that the Education Department "not seek to fund any specific additional analyses from the Longitudinal or Immersion studies." Despite this evidence, the National Association for Bilingual Education, or NABE, had the gall to claim that the NAS review "validated" these two studies and bilingual education.

Professor Christine Rossell of Boston University recently

Mike Ritter. Reprinted by special permission of North America Syndicate.

completed an extensive review of more than 300 bilingual-education studies. She found that out of only 60 methodologically acceptable studies measuring reading ability, 78 percent found bilingual education to be no better or actually worse than doing nothing. In terms of math scores, 91 percent of only 34 scientifically valid studies showed bilingual education to be no better or worse than doing nothing. After visiting dozens of bilingual classes, Rossell found that those few bilingual programs that do work do so only because they subvert the theory and do not waste time trying to teach children to read and write in any language other than English. She has recommended that the best program for language-minority children is immersion in English in a class with a specially trained teacher who may use their native language only when really necessary.

A LONELY BATTLE

In spite of the evidence, Latino parents who oppose bilingual education often find themselves fighting a lonely battle. In fact, parent groups in Los Angeles and New York are being assisted by local religious organizations and not traditional Hispanic advocacy or civil-rights groups. Lacking a racial identity to unify diverse Hispanic groups around the country, Latino activists rely on Spanish to fulfill this function. Latino activists may believe it is in their material interests to maintain the Spanish language of their constituency rather than help them assimilate and learn English. Despite their attempts, professional Latino lobbyists have not convinced a majority of Hispanics that bilingual education is better for their children. Surveys show that the overwhelming majority of immigrants believe it is a family's duty, and not the school's, to help children maintain their native language. When Mexican and Cuban parents were asked their opinion in an Education Department survey, four-fifths declared their opposition to teaching children in Spanish if it meant less time devoted to English. With more than 20 million immigrants in the United States, it's more important than ever to teach newcomers to speak English and to think of themselves as Americans if we hope to remain one people, not simply a conglomeration of different groups. It is time for federal and state legislators to overhaul bilingual education. Clearly, the best policy for children—and for the country—is to teach English to immigrant and nonimmigrant children as quickly as possible.

PERIODICAL BIBLIOGRAPHY

The following articles have been selected to supplement the diverse views presented in this chapter. Addresses are provided for periodicals not indexed in the *Readers' Guide to Periodical Literature*, the *Alternative Press Index*, the *Social Sciences Index*, or the *Index to Legal Periodicals and Books*.

American Scholar	Forum on teaching American history, Winter 1998.
Martin K. Anderson	"Achieving Libre: An Interview with Martin Espada," Z *Magazine*, December 1998.
Julian E. Barnes	"A Surprising Turn on Minority Enrollments," *U.S. News & World Report*, January 5, 1998.
Edgar F. Beckham	"Diversity Opens Doors to All," *New York Times*, January 5, 1997.
Estela Mara Bensimon and Marta Soto	"Can We Rebuild Civic Life Without a Multiracial University?" *Change*, January/February 1997.
Linda Chavez	"Multiculturalism Is Driving Us Apart," *USA Today*, May 1996.
John Fonte	"We the Peoples," *National Review*, March 25, 1996.
John Gallagher	"Multiculturalism at a Crossroads," *Education Digest*, April 1998.
Keith Gilyard and Nicholas Stix	"Would Ebonics Programs in Public Schools Be a Good Idea?" *Insight*, March 31, 1997. Available from 3600 New York Ave. NE, Washington, DC, 20002.
Christine Granados	"Admissions Test," *Hispanic*, April 1998. Available from PO Box 15879, North Hollywood, CA 91615-9737.
Issues and Controversies On File	"Bilingual Education," September 12, 1997. Available from Facts On File News Services, 11 Penn Plaza, New York, NY 10001-2006.
Elizabeth Martinez	"Reinventing 'America,'" Z *Magazine*, December 1996.
Newsweek	"Makeup Test: More History, Less P.C.," April 15, 1996.
Theresa Perry and Lisa Delpit, eds.	Special issue on Ebonics, *Rethinking Schools*, Fall 1997.
Anthony M. Platt	"End Game: The Rise and Fall of Affirmative Action in Higher Education," *Social Justice*, Summer 1997.

CHAPTER 4

WHAT ROLE SHOULD RELIGIOUS AND MORAL VALUES PLAY IN PUBLIC EDUCATION?

CHAPTER PREFACE

Many social observers and analysts report that moral corruption and character problems are on the rise among high school and college students. "Although many young persons demonstrate a higher moral consciousness—greater commitment to human rights, concern about the environment, and global awareness—than previous generations, the general youth trends present a darker picture," declares education professor Thomas Lickona. An increasing amount of selfishness, cheating, stealing, high rates of unplanned pregnancy, startling incidents of violence, and a growing disrespect for authority seen among today's students have prompted many parents and educators to take part in the "character education" movement.

Advocates of character education contend that basic moral principles must be taught in schools. Currently, the thousands of institutions (about 20 percent of U.S. schools) participating in this movement use widely varying approaches to teaching values. Some schools require students to take courses in ethics and character development; others present values lessons during homerooms and assemblies; still others emphasize specific works of literature, philosophy, and theology to teach moral basics. Inevitably, all schools promote some sort of values system through the behavior of their educators, argues Virginia teacher Patricia Giegerich: "What you don't teach is just as important as what you teach. . . . And if you ignore values or ethical issues as something you can't talk about, you're teaching nonetheless. You're saying they're not important."

Critics, however, fear that public schools could use character education to promote values contrary to parents' beliefs. Both conservatives and liberals are concerned about what slant character educators would take when faced with controversial issues such as abortion, sex education, and homosexuality. Even discussing seemingly noncontroversial values, such as tolerance and justice, could be problematic. As commentator David Carlin puts it: "*Whose* values will be taught[?] . . .Values of self-expression or self-control? Values rooted in religion or secularism?" Others question whether it is wise to allow state institutions to teach morality. A reader responding to a 1995 *New York Times Magazine* article on character education wrote, "Do you suppose that if [Nazi] Germany had had character education . . . it would have encouraged children to fight Nazism or support it?"

Whether schools can and should teach ethical values is one of the subjects debated by the authors in the following chapter.

"Schools at all levels can do a lot to improve the moral climate in our society."

SCHOOLS SHOULD TEACH MORAL VALUES

Christina Hoff Sommers

In more than a dozen U.S. states, educators are participating in the "character education" movement—a push to teach moral values in schools. Critics of this movement contend that schools could impose beliefs contrary to those taught in the home. In the following viewpoint, Christina Hoff Sommers argues that schools should teach moral values. She maintains that teachers must use history and literature to teach uncontroversial moral principles such as honesty, integrity, and sacrifice. Because these principles are part of the nation's moral heritage, America's children have a right to learn them in school, she concludes. Sommers teaches philosophy at Clark University in Worcester, Massachusetts. She is also a resident fellow at the American Enterprise Institute, a conservative research organization.

As you read, consider the following questions:

1. What is the proof that today's students are "basically decent," in Sommers' opinion?
2. According to the author, how do students often respond to the assertion that genocide is evil?
3. What is Sommers' definition of "moral conservationism?"

Excerpted from Christina Hoff Sommers, "To Lead and Live," St. Croix Review, June 1998. Reprinted by permission of the author.

For the past fifteen years I have taught moral philosophy at Clark University. I have written about character education and ethics for popular and professional journals. I have visited many colleges and prep schools talking to students about ethics. I will give you the best information I have on the state of moral education in America. That includes the good as well as the bizarre.

I am persuaded that schools at all levels can do a lot to improve the moral climate in our society: they can do a lot to help restore civility and community if they commit themselves to this and have the courage to act. On the other hand, they can also continue to do very little, thereby fostering a climate of cynicism and moral relativism. How can we make our moral education more effective?

A MORAL HAZE

When you have as many conversations as I do with young people, you come away both exhilarated and depressed. As I am sure most of you are aware as parents, teachers, administrators, and students—there is a great deal of simple goodheartedness, instinctive fair-mindedness, and spontaneous generosity of spirit in our young people. Most of the students in my own classes, or those I encounter in the high schools, and colleges I visit, strike me as being basically decent. They form wonderful friendships, they seem to be considerate of and grateful to their parents—more than the baby boomers were. (In many ways contemporary young people are more likable than the baby boomers—less fascinated with themselves, more able to laugh at themselves). An astonishing number of them are doing volunteer work (seventy percent of college students, according to the one annual survey of freshman attitudes). They are donating blood to Red Cross in record numbers, they deliver food to housebound elderly people. They spend part of their summer vacation working with deaf children or doing volunteer work in Mexico. This is a generation of kids that, with relatively little guidance and religious training, is doing some very concrete and effective things for other people.

But conceptually and culturally, today's young people live in a moral haze. Ask one of them if there even is such a thing as right and wrong and suddenly you are confronted with a confused, tongue-tied, nervous, and insecure individual. The same person who works weekends for Meals on Wheels or who volunteers for a suicide prevention hotline or a domestic violence shelter might tell you: "Well, there really is no such thing as right or wrong. It's kind of like what works best for the individual. Each person has to work it out for himself." Ladies and gentlemen: that kind of answer, which is so common as to be typical, is no better than the moral philosophy of a sociopath.

I often find students incapable of making even one single confident moral judgment. The talk inevitably reverts to Adolf Hitler and the Nazis. So you tell them that Hitler was morally depraved. You state the thesis that torturing human beings is wrong or that genocide is unambiguously evil. But then these excruciatingly tolerant students get this glaze in their eyes and reply, "Who are we to say? We can't really be a judge of others. We consider hurting people wrong in our society. But all that means is that it's wrong for us, but perhaps not for others.". . .

A Distrust of Objectivity

The notion of objective moral truths is in disrepute. Unsurprisingly, this mistrust of objectivity has begun to spill over to other areas of knowledge. Today, the idea of objective truth in science and history is also being impugned. For there has been an assault on the very notion of objective fact. Wendy Shalit, an undergraduate at Williams College, recently reported that her classmates, who had been taught that "all knowledge is a social construct," are doubtful that the Holocaust ever occurred. One of her classmates said, "Though the Holocaust may not have happened, it's a perfectly reasonable conceptual hallucination."

In effect, we are raising a generation of young people who are not being given the arguments to support the ideals by which most of them instinctively live. They are morally inarticulate. For it is today fashionable to cast doubt on what is objectively obvious and to denigrate the truths of morality by which decent people live and love. By the same token it has become unfashionable to defend those truths. It is especially unfashionable to defend them with passion. . . .

The Great Relearning

What is to be done? How can we improve young people's knowledge and understanding of moral history? How can we restore young people's confidence in the great moral ideals? How can we help them become morally articulate, morally literate, self-confident?

I have a few ideas to suggest to you some of which came to me recently as I was reading some entertaining passages in one of my favorite contemporary social critics, Tom Wolfe.

In the late sixties a group of hippies living in the Haight-Ashbury District of San Francisco decided that hygiene was a middle class hang-up that they could best do without. So they lived without it. For example, baths and showers, while not actually banned, were frowned upon as retrograde practices. The essayist and novelist Tom Wolfe was intrigued by these hippies who he said "sought nothing less than to sweep aside all codes and restraints of the past and start out from zero."

At the Haight-Ashbury Free Clinic there were doctors who were treating diseases no living doctor had ever encountered before, diseases that had disappeared so long ago they had never even picked up Latin names, diseases such as the mange, the grunge, the itch, the twitch, the thrush, the scroff, the rot.

The itching and the manginess eventually began to vex the hippies, leading them individually to seek help from the local free clinic. Step by step, they had to rediscover, for themselves, the rudiments of modern hygiene. Wolfe refers to it as the "Great Relearning." The Great Relearning is what has to happen whenever earnest reformers extirpate too much, whenever, "starting from zero," they jettison basic social practices and institutions, abandoning common routines, defying common sense, reason, conventional wisdom—and, sometimes, sanity itself. . . .

MORAL CONSERVATION

We need our own Great Relearning. I am going to propose a few ideas on how we might carry out this relearning. I am going to propose something that could be called moral conservationism. We are born into a moral environment just as we are born into a natural environment. Just as there are basic environmental necessities; clear air, safe food, fresh water, there are basic moral necessities. What is a society like without civility, honesty, considerateness, self-discipline? Without a population educated to civility, educated to be considerate and respectful of one another, what will we end up with? Not much. As long as philosophers and theologians have been writing about ethics they have stressed the moral basics. We live in a moral environment. We have to respect it and protect it. We have to acquaint our children with it. We have to make them aware that it is precious and fragile.

I have suggestions for some specific reforms. They are far from being revolutionary, indeed some are pretty obvious. They are common sense, but we live in an age when common sense is becoming increasingly hard to come by.

We must encourage and honor those teachers who accept the responsibility of providing a classical moral education for their students. The last few decades of the twentieth century has seen a steady erosion of knowledge and steady increase in moral skepticism. It is partly due to the diffidence of many teachers confused by all the talk about pluralism. Such teachers actually believe that it is not right to "indoctrinate" our children in their own culture and moral tradition. But of course all cultures pass on their moral teachings to their young. Why should contemporary America be the exception?

DEFINING RIGHT AND WRONG

In its underlying philosophy, character education rejects moral relativism and reasserts the idea of objective morality—the notion that some things are truly right and others wrong. Character educators typically define right and wrong in terms of "core ethical values" such as respect, responsibility, honesty, caring, fairness, and self-control. They argue that these core values have objective moral worth because they are good for the individual, good for schools, good for society, and consistent with universal moral principles such as the Golden Rule. When we do not act in accord with these basic values, we create problems for ourselves and others.

Thomas Lickona, *World & I*, June 1996.

I recently saw a PBS special on ethics in the classroom. There were interviews with a group of high school kids from New Hampshire who were not sure why cheating was wrong. Some of the kids were in gangs and admitted to doing a lot of antisocial things. The parents seemed to agree character education in schools was necessary. But then the documentary showed that it was not going to be easy: the parents could not reach a consensus on several controversial moral topics. The teachers and parents sounded confused, diffident, unsure, helpless, or worse. Some thought moral education meant defending a very progressive agenda: gay rights and abortion rights; others thought it meant just the opposite: defending old-fashioned family values. These parents were very much against any talk of gay rights and abortion rights. The message of the PBS special was this: character education may be a good idea; but there may be no way to do it in our pluralistic, tolerant society in which everyone has his own idea about right and wrong.

As I was watching the program I felt like calling the station to ask them to stop the tape. For there is far more consensus than the program allowed. Of course there are pressing moral issues around which there is no consensus. As a modern pluralistic society we are arguing about gay rights, assisted suicide, and abortion. That is understandable. New moral dilemmas arise in every generation. But we have long ago achieved consensus on other basic moral questions. Cheating, cowardice, and cruelty are wrong. As one pundit put it, "The Commandments are not the ten highly tentative suggestions." While it is true that our society must debate such controversial issues as capital punishment, assisted suicide, etc., we must not forget that there are also the core of uncontroversial ethical issues that were settled a long time ago. Read the Bible, read Aristotle's Ethics, read Shakespeare's King Lear—read the Koran, or the Analects of Confucius, read almost any great work and you encounter the uncontroversial moral basics: integrity, respect for human life, self-control, honesty and sacrifice. All of the world's major religions proffer some version of the Golden Rule if only in its negative forms: not to do unto others as we should not have them do unto us. Is there anyone who seriously doubts this principle? Why are so few defending and actively teaching this simple and powerful moral principle? . . .

THE RIGHT TO A MORAL HERITAGE

I am not saying that a good literary education is sufficient to create morally sensitive human beings; but keeping children ignorant of their moral heritage is one way to get ourselves a generation of morally shortchanged human beings. Children who are basically honest but who have not been taught and so don't know that lying and cheating are wrong or cannot say why they are wrong; children who are compassionate but who aren't sure that cruelty in exotic societies is just as wrong as it is in our own. Such students are being cheated of their moral heritage that is the glory of our nation. For all our children are rightful heirs to the Judeo-Christian tradition and the European Enlightenment that taught our Founding Fathers their morals and their politics. It is a heritage to which they have a right and which should be respectfully handed over to them by our educational system. . . .

We need to bring the great books and the great ideas back into the center of the curriculum. We need to transmit the best of our political and cultural heritage. We need to hold back on the cynical attacks on our traditions and institutions. We need to expose the folly of all the schemes for starting from zero. We need to teach our young people to understand, to respect and to protect the institutions that protect us and preserve our humane, free and democratic society. This we can do. This we must do. And when we engage in the great relearning that is so badly needed today, we will find that the center of our free community is holding and is strong. The lives of our children will then be safer, saner, more dignified, more humane, for we shall then be truly "educating to live and lead in a civil society."

| "Will the schools teach liberal or conservative values? Values of self-expression or self-control? Values rooted in religion or in secularism?"

SCHOOLS CANNOT TEACH MORAL VALUES

David R. Carlin

Supporters of the "character education" movement contend that moral values should be taught in public schools. In the following viewpoint, David R. Carlin maintains that U.S. schools cannot effectively teach moral values. Because American society encompasses groups of people that support widely varying value systems, schools are unable to teach values without alienating some sector of the public. Carlin is a columnist for *Commonweal*, a biweekly Catholic periodical.

As you read, consider the following questions:
1. According to Carlin, what do parents usually mean when they ask schools to teach moral values?
2. How can the teaching of abstract principles such as fairness become a problem, in the author's opinion?
3. In what way can values rooted in the U.S. Constitution become divisive, in Carlin's view?

Reprinted from David R. Carlin, "Teaching Values in School: Which Ones? Whose?" *Commonweal*, February 9, 1996, by permission of *Commonweal*.

There is much talk nowadays about the need for public schools to teach moral values. In a society which, for thirty years, has been drifting downriver toward the Niagara of moral anarchy, there is no doubt about it: somebody needs to teach moral values to the young. But can the public schools do it? I doubt it.

Leaving aside a number of other difficulties, let's focus on the vexed question of *whose* values will be taught. Will the schools teach liberal or conservative values? Values of self-expression or self-control? Values rooted in religion or in secularism? Values of individual autonomy or of community?

A SENSIBLE APPROACH TO TEACHING VALUES?

Now there happens to be a standard way of trying to meet this difficulty. It is argued (by former secretary of education Bill Bennett, for one) that, no matter what our moral disagreements, all Americans share many important values. We may, for instance, disagree about sexual questions. But so what? Sex, after all, isn't the whole of morality. Everyone agrees that fairness, honesty, courage, and respect for others are good qualities, while unfairness, dishonesty, cowardice, and disrespect are bad. These lists of noncontroversial good and bad qualities, these virtues and vices, can easily be extended. We agree, for instance, on certain values enshrined in the United States Constitution: the rule of law, a republican form of government, democracy, due process, equal protection, freedoms of speech, press, assembly, religion, etc. So let schools teach a broad range of noncontroversial values while maintaining a prudent silence about the narrow range of controversial questions.

Note well, we are told, that this sensible policy does not mean that children will learn nothing about controversial matters. Far from it. Parents, churches, and other nonschool agencies of socialization will be quite free to give instruction on such issues. According, then, to this common-sense division of labor, schools will teach fairness and the Bill of Rights while parents and churches will teach about adolescent sex. The Smith family and their local Southern Baptist church will teach abstinence, while the Jones family and their local Unitarian church will teach safe sex.

THE DEVIL IS IN THE DETAILS

As an abstract proposal, this seems reasonable. But as usual, the devil is in the details.

Take teen sex, for instance. Most parents already teach that this is wrong, especially for girls. But to judge from sociological survey data, not to mention sky-high rates of adolescent pregnancy and sexually transmitted diseases, such teaching is often not very efficacious. We hear parents say they would like schools to teach "moral values." Translate this into English, and you'll find that what they usually mean is that they want the schools to help them in the difficult job of inculcating sexual restraint in their kids. A values curriculum that keeps silent about adolescent sex will evoke this response from parents: "So what's the point? If you don't plan to say anything about teen sex, why are you doing this at all?"

THE PROBLEM WITH CHARACTER EDUCATION

On both the left and the right, there is concern that character education could touch on issues that bitterly divide Americans. "We believe teaching civility is a great virtue, but if included in that is, 'You must accept homosexuality as a valid alternative lifestyle,' then it's problematic," says Perry Glanzer, education policy analyst at Focus on the Family, a conservative Christian group in Colorado Springs, Colo. . . .

At the other end of the political spectrum, the American Civil Liberties Union (ACLU) worries that character education could pose constitutional problems, though the organization cannot cite any instances of violations. "It really depends on whether you're talking about a thinly veiled way of getting religious, ethical and moral issues into the classroom that are not seen by the entire population as American civic values, or you're talking about good citizenship, fairness, tolerance—those sorts of things," says Loren Siegel, the ACLU's director of public education.

"I would be very surprised if there weren't problems," Siegel adds. "Not everyone believes a fetus is a human being or that children should always be obedient and never question authority."

Sarah Glazer, CQ Researcher, June 21, 1996.

But if the schools rise to this challenge and decide to tackle the sex question, they're right back in their original quandary. Should they take an "abstinence" approach or a "safe sex" approach? If the latter, they'll outrage moral and religious conservatives; if the former, they'll outrage moral liberals and secularists.

PRINCIPLES IN PRACTICE

Or consider fairness. We all believe in fairness as an abstract principle, but what does it mean in practice? What does it mean, for instance, when applied to divorce? Or when applied to social policy questions, like affirmative action, food stamps, Medicare? Or when applied to abortion and euthanasia? If the essence of fairness is respect for the rights of others, then everything depends on what rights others actually have. But this question of rights, like sex, is highly controversial. Some people favor this list of human rights, some that list, others a third.

Maybe the schools will respond to this dilemma by saying: "Our fairness curriculum will teach kids not to cut in line and not to steal one another's pencils; but we'll take no stand on divisive questions like divorce, social policy, abortion, and euthanasia." But this is tantamount to teaching that fairness applies to small matters only, not to big matters. Once again, what's the point?

Alternatively, the schools might say: "On controversial questions like divorce, affirmative action, etc., we'll teach nothing as to *content*, but we'll teach a *method* of approaching the issues." But which method? It is not just moral answers that are controversial; so are methods of answering moral questions. Some people search the Scriptures. Some consult the new Catholic catechism. Some rely on intuition. Some look for help from social scientists (who are in notorious disagreement among themselves). Most simply adopt the prejudices of their social peers. Whichever method schools adopt, they will give offense.

DIVISIVE CONSTITUTIONAL ISSUES

At first glance, teaching values enshrined in the U.S. Constitution seems promising—until we remember that the most divisive issue in the nation today is the question of abortion. The Supreme Court says the Constitution includes a right to abortion. But according to many legal scholars plus a large and intense section of public opinion, it includes nothing of the sort. As they see it, the 1973 *Roe* decision was a constitutional bonehead play. So what are the schools to say about this?

Perhaps, making the usual move, they will say: "We'll note in passing that the abortion question is highly debatable, but we'll focus our attention on nondebatable aspects of the Constitution, like trial by jury, *habeas corpus*, etc." To which I can imagine a morally conservative parent replying: "Thanks for nothing. My real worry is that my daughter Susie, growing up in a society in which the Supreme Court condones abortion, may someday decide to kill her unborn child. I am not worried that she may someday decide to abolish *habeas corpus*."

Schools can be effective moral teachers when they represent communities that are morally homogeneous. The trouble is, American society is no longer a morally homogeneous community.

"A nation that denies God in our schools is a nation that encourages the devil in our schools."

SCHOOL-SPONSORED PRAYER SHOULD BE ALLOWED

Ann Donnelly

Ann Donnelly is an energy consultant and a former chair of the Clark County, Washington, Republican party. In the following viewpoint, Donnelly contends that voluntary student-led prayer should be allowed during school hours. Currently, student-led prayer is allowed before and after school hours, but vocal prayer during school hours has been banned by the U.S. Supreme Court. The author maintains that voluntary school-supported prayer—including prayers of the major non-Christian religions—would help to stem the tide of violence and illegal activity seen in many of the nation's public schools.

As you read, consider the following questions:
1. In Donnelly's opinion, what can happen to students who have a spiritual void in their lives?
2. According to Donnelly, why would voluntary school prayer not create a "monopoly for Christianity?"
3. What alternative school activities are currently available for students who want to express their religious views, according to the author?

Reprinted from Ann Donnelly, "Classroom Prayer Would Be Preferable," *The Columbian*, April 12, 1998, by permission of the author.

S tudents organizing voluntary prayer groups at Mountain View and Columbia River high schools in Washington state are doing their part to make their schools more positive places to learn.

Similarly, the teachers who agree to monitor the groups are using their scant personal time for a worthy purpose: filling the spiritual void in students' lives that, if neglected, could draw them toward violence, drugs or gangs.

Mayhem in schools is escalating. Late in March 1998, two Jonesboro, Ark. middle-schoolers massacred four of their school-mates and a heroic teacher. A week later, a 12-year-old boy who fancied himself "Mr. Pimp" was accused of running a prostitution ring in his middle-school class. In April 1998, a 15-year-old was expelled from an Ohio school for compiling an electronic "hit list" of students and teachers. During the same month, an Idaho student reportedly held students and administrators hostage, threatening to kill them if authorities did not bring him vodka and whiskey.

So when local students gather voluntarily to pray and discuss the role of faith in making them stronger, we should honor them.

A CONTENTIOUS ISSUE

Will voluntary school prayer, currently allowed only before and after school, be expanded to include school hours? That is the hope of supporters of a proposed constitutional amendment, the Religious Freedom Act, currently before the U.S. House of Representatives.

The issue has long been among our society's most contentious. In 1963, a landmark U.S. Supreme Court ruling banned school-sponsored prayer and Bible readings. Fearing expensive litigation, many schools went beyond the ruling's requirements and banned all religious expression. Since then, policies have loosened somewhat to allow voluntary student-led prayer groups such as the ones at Mountain View and Columbia River high schools.

In the spring of 1998 the full House will vote on House Joint Resolution 78, the first step in a long process for the proposed constitutional amendment. The resolution has 150 sponsors, including Washington congresswomen Linda Smith and Jennifer Dunn.

According to Rep. Smith, the measure would "ensure that religious expression is kept on a level playing field with all other types of expression." If the measure succeeds in its long process of approval, it would permit voluntary, student-led prayers during the school day so long as school administrators do not write, require or forbid the prayers.

SUPPORTING ALL MAJOR RELIGIONS

Can something completely voluntary become tyrannical? *The Columbian* believes so. In an April 7, 1998, editorial, "Amendment Imposes What Founders Escaped," the newspaper describes the proposed amendment as a step toward "theocracy" and recommends it be resisted fiercely. Supporters of the amendment "don't want religious freedom," the editorial contends, but rather want to establish a virtual monopoly for Christianity.

The latter complaint is a stretch. Observant Muslims and Jews have also clashed with authorities in schools and universities, and would benefit from the more tolerant and entirely voluntary policies. Those of us who know Dunn and Smith are confident of their support for voluntary prayers from students of all the major religions.

Reprinted by permission of Steve Kelley.

Furthermore, compared to pimping, massacres, hostage-takings and planned assassinations in schools, the degree of theocracy represented by voluntary school prayer might represent an improvement.

In a March 30, 1998, speech on the House floor, Democratic

Rep. James Traficant of Ohio made virtually the same point: "Schools are overrun with drugs, violence, guns, rape, murder, and now even mass murder. It seems America's schools have everything except prayer.

"Maybe the so-called experts might finally realize that a nation that denies God in our schools is a nation that encourages the devil in our schools."

THE NEED FOR RELIGIOUS WISDOM

Millions of Americans would agree with Traficant, but the political reality is not encouraging. Traficant, Smith, Dunn and their fellow supporters cannot guarantee the success of their constitutional amendment. [In June 1998, the Religious Freedom Amendment failed in the House of Representatives.]

Fortunately, in the meantime, students wishing to express their religious views in school have available a range of activities already allowed by the Supreme Court. In its landmark ruling in the early 1960s, the Supreme Court stated that public education should include "a study of comparative religion or the history of religion," thus permitting a variety of voluntary expressions.

The more the better, so long as such expressions are voluntary and constitutional.

The wisdom of the world's great religions helps kids deal with tragedies such as Jonesboro, Ark., after they occur. Perhaps the same wisdom can help prevent violence from occurring in the first place.

> "The law with respect to school prayer is clear: when organized, supported, or required by the state, school prayer is illegal."

SCHOOL-SPONSORED PRAYER IS UNCONSTITUTIONAL

Tom Peters, Jim Allison, and Susan Batte

In the following viewpoint, Tom Peters, Jim Allison, and Susan Batte contend that any public school–sponsored prayer is illegal. Because the U.S. Constitution forbids the government to enact a religious practice, school-supported prayer cannot be allowed. Moreover, the authors point out, students attending public schools have the right not to participate in prayer that may contradict their beliefs. Peters is a professor of communications at the University of Louisville in Kentucky. Allison is an independent researcher living in Virginia Beach, Virginia. Batte is a lawyer in Norfolk, Virginia.

As you read, consider the following questions:

1. What sparked the 1963 *Engel v. Vitale* Supreme Court case?
2. According to Peters, Allison, and Batte, what is the problem with the suggestion that prayers could be rotated among the various religious faiths?
3. What type of prayer remains legal in the public schools, according to the authors?

Reprinted, with permission, from Tom Peters, Jim Allison, and Susan Batte, "Is Government-Supported Prayer Constitutional?" 1997 web publication found at www.louisville.edu/~tnpete01/church/pray3.htm.

The law with respect to school prayer is clear: when organized, supported, or required by the state, school prayer is illegal. Our purpose in this viewpoint is to explain . . . why this is the case.

Briefly, state-supported prayer amounts to the establishment of a religious practice. This is true whether the state actually prescribes the prayer to be said, or allows teachers and students to compose the prayer as they see fit. Let's use the famous 1963 *Engel v. Vitale* case to illustrate our argument.

Engel v. Vitale revolved around a New York law that required school officials to publically recite each school day the following prayer, composed by the New York Board of Regents: "Almighty God, we acknowledge our dependence upon Thee, and we beg Thy blessings upon us, our parents, our teachers, and our country."

The Court ruled, correctly in our opinion, that the New York law violated the First Amendment. Indeed it's difficult to imagine how the Court could have ruled otherwise. Prayer is, without question, a religious exercise, and when the state requires that a prayer be recited, it is establishing a religious practice. Additionally, it violates free exercise for the state to expose students to prayer against their will, or to force students to absent themselves from the classroom to avoid a prayer they do not want to hear. Finally, we note that, despite the fact that this prayer was written to be as general and non-sectarian as possible, it *still* establishes religious beliefs, beliefs that surely do not reflect the religious sensibilities of many students. Christians, for example, might justifiably complain that the prayer is not offered in the name of Christ, while polytheists and adherents to new-age religions might have problems with the implied assertion that there is a single God, or that this God is almighty. And non-theists would certainly object to repeating words that imply that they are "dependent" on a God in which they do not believe. No matter how charitably one views the facts of *Engel v. Vitale*, it is difficult to escape the conclusion that the Regents' prayer would not be acceptable to many students.

ARGUMENTS AND FACTS

In our e-mail and usenet correspondence we have heard a number of arguments about why prayers of the *Engel v. Vitale* sort either do not violate the Constitution, or can be made to not violate the Constitution. Let's look at some of the more important of these arguments:

• *The students can be excused from prayer.* True, but this doesn't resolve the Constitutional problem. The state establishes a religious practice when it orders that prayer be said, *regardless* of whether people attend the prayer. Moreover, this is hardly an effective way of resolving the problem. On the contrary, such excusal would publicly single out students who refuse to take part in prayer. As many have observed, children ostracize people who are different from themselves. Additionally, the nature of excusal is to make children feel as if they are not doing something that would otherwise be expected of them, i.e., it sends the message that the state considers prayer to be "normal" and "routine."

• *Students that don't want to pray can simply sit silently.* But this doesn't solve anything either; if religious liberty means anything, it is that I choose when and how to expose myself to religious practices. If I don't want to be exposed to prayer, why should I be required to listen to it? Imagine, for example, that a judge ordered me, as part of a parole agreement, to attend a Catholic Church every Sunday. Without question, this order would violate my religious liberty—it forces me to attend a church not of my choice at the order of the state. It would be nonsense to argue that the order is constitutional on the grounds that I don't actually have to take communion or otherwise participate in the religious service. Neither is it constitutional to force children to listen to prayers in which they do not want to participate.

• *The State doesn't have to write the prayer; teachers can make one up on their own, or students can decide among themselves.* Again, this wouldn't solve the constitutional problem. It is just as illegal to order a teacher to compose a prayer as it is for the state to write one; either way students end up listening to a prayer they may not want to hear at the behest of the state. And it surely violates the religious liberty of teachers to force them to compose prayers by law, or to limit the content of these prayers. Conversely, if *no* limitation is placed on what can be said, prayer will become an open invitation to evangelism in the classroom.

It is equally unconstitutional to have children "choose among themselves." It is of no consequence to the Constitution that students write or select the prayer they say; so long as that prayer is required by the state, it's unconstitutional. There are practical problems as well. It's nonsense, for example, to think that first or second graders will have the theological sophistication to compose prayers of their own. Further, there is no guarantee that student-composed prayer will reflect the religious beliefs of all students. On the contrary, such prayers would be just as open to abuse as teacher-led prayer. Finally, students are *already* free to meet together and pray before class if they want to, so long as the state plays no role in organizing the prayer.

THE STATE CANNOT REQUIRE PRAYER

• *We can rotate prayers among the faiths represented in the class.* Not and still be constitutional. Rotated or not, when the state orders that a prayer will be said, it establishes a religious practice. Additionally, such proposals are fraught with problems. First, rotating prayers guarantees that prayers will be sectarian (if generic prayers are acceptable, why rotate prayers?). And if prayers are said in proportion to the number of students in class who hold a particular faith, students that adhere to minority religions will have their prayers said very infrequently, while "majority" prayers will be heard every week. This will do nothing more than reinforce the minority status of minority religions. Finally, there is nothing equivalent to prayer in the non-theist community. Will atheists be included the rotation? If not, how will their views be represented?

• *Prayer does not establish a religion.* Correct. It establishes a religious practice, which is just as illegal. The First Amendment does not proscribe the establishment of *a* religion; it proscribes establishment of religion generally. It is no more correct to argue that the state can require prayer so long as that prayer is non-sectarian than it is correct to argue that the state can require that you attend a religious service once a month so long as the state does not designate the service you have to attend.

• *It doesn't harm a kid to have him/her pray.* True, but that doesn't make it legal. Besides, "harm" is in the eye of the beholder. An atheist might very well consider it harmful to expose kids to religious doctrines he/she considers false and destructive. Similarly, in the years before *Engel v. Vitale* Catholic parents definitely considered it harmful when their children were asked to recite the Protestant version of the Lord's prayer, or were asked to read from the King James Version of the Bible which, to Catholic tastes, is translated incorrectly.

PROHIBITING PRAYER IS APPROPRIATE

• *Even if you're technically right, it just goes too far to proscribe simple prayers.* On the contrary, the simple prayers proscribed in the 1960s were the source of profound discomfort by many students in the years before *Engel*. As noted above, most Bible reading was from the King James Bible, and many prayers had a Protestant "feel" to them, which infuriated Catholics. Jews were offended at being forced to read from the New Testament of any Bible. Non-believers disliked the whole idea of being forced to participate in prayer. Even some religious Protestants disliked praying "generic" prayers that did not express their beliefs. The *Engel* decision was a completely appropriate remedy for what had long been a bothersome government intrusion into the private lives of its citizens.

• *Proscribing prayer deprives parents of their right to have prayer if they want it.* No it doesn't. Prayer remains completely legal in the public schools. A parent can still instruct a child to pray in the tradition of his or her family, and teachers must legally respect the student's right to pray so long as those prayers do not disrupt the educational mission of the schools. On the contrary, the only thing limited by proscribing organized prayer in the schools is the rights of some parents to determine what *other* kids will have to pray.

• *Why not just set aside a time for prayer in the morning and let kids pray as they want?* Generally, such proposals are legal, so long as the time is not set aside exclusively for prayer. Moment of silence laws, for example, have been found to be legal by the Supreme Court. But if the statute sets the time aside for prayer, it amounts to the state favoring prayer over other activities, and further declares that prayer is an appropriate activity at certain times and places in the school day. The state has no right to do either of these things.

In summary, organized school prayer is unconstitutional for perfectly good reasons. You don't have to be a legal scholar to understand why it's wrong for the state to organize prayer. When the state forces you to pray, it is forcing you to participate in a religious practice. That amounts to establishment of religion, and that's unconstitutional.

| "When the State protects
evolutionary interpretations and
theories from intelligent criticism,
the State is ... violating the Free
Exercise rights of the student who
believes in creation."

SCIENTIFIC EVIDENCE AGAINST EVOLUTION AND FOR CREATION SHOULD BE INCLUDED IN SCIENCE CURRICULA

Robert E. Kofahl

In the following viewpoint, Robert E. Kofahl argues that creation science—the theory that the origins of life are the result of purposeful divine action—should be included in public school science curricula. The theory of evolution—the idea that life developed through a process of mutations and natural selection—should not be taught as scientific fact because it has not been proven. Evolutionary theory should instead be treated as a hypothesis subject to critical evaluation and competing ideas, Kofahl contends. Kofahl holds a doctorate in chemistry and is the science coordinator for the Creation Science Research Center in San Diego, California. He is also coauthor of *The Creation Explanation*.

As you read, consider the following questions:

1. In Kofahl's opinion, what are the core competing principles of evolution and creation?
2. What are the primary assumptions of creation science, according to the author?

Adapted from Appendix 2 and Appendix 3 of *The Handy Dandy Evolution Refuter*, by Robert E. Kofahl, at www.parentcompany.com/handy_dandy/hder-rek.htm. Reprinted with permission from the author.

1. Evolutionary interpretations and theories are taught:
   a. Dogmatically as facts of earth history,
   b. Protectively, without criticism of weaknesses and failures,
   c. Exclusively, without competition, as the only scientifically acceptable way of thinking about the world.
   d. Under an erroneous definition of science that is distorted by the injection of belief in a totally materialistic, uncreated universe as a prerequisite to valid scientific thought or research.

2. This is wrong because:
   a. It is poor science.
      • There is no place for dogma in science. What cannot be demonstrated to be fact should not be taught as fact.
      • Theories in science should not be protected. They must always be open to critical evaluation.
      • All ideas in science should be open to competition with alternative ideas.
      • Science, properly defined, is a method of studying the natural order, not a belief system about it.
   b. It is poor teaching methodology to stifle criticism or competition of ideas.
   c. Dogmatic, protective, exclusive teaching of evolution denies to Christians and other religious students their constitutionally guaranteed right to the free exercise of their faith.

How Origins Interpretations Should Be Taught

1. The observable, reproducible scientific data should be clearly distinguished from theories, interpretations and speculative historical scenarios.

2. Students should understand that in interpreting scientific data:
   a. Science correctly defined does not require scientists to believe in a materialistic universe that is closed off from divine activity and intervention.
   b. It is no less "scientific" to believe in creation rather than in evolution.
   c. The core competing principles of evolution and creation are the origin of biological designs, respectively, (1) by spontaneous materialistic processes or (2) by intelligent purposeful design. (Note: "Spontaneous" means without any input of intelligence, purpose, plan, design, goal, etc.)

d. It is proper in science to consider the evidence for and against both explanations for the origin of biodesigns.

3. The assumptions basic to each interpretation should be clearly understood. They are:

  a. For evolution

- That spontaneous materialistic processes produced all characteristics of all organisms.
- That all species are related by descent from one or a few common ancestors.
- That biological variation has in effect been unlimited (i.e., from amoeba to university professor in just 3 billion years.)

  b. For creation

- That the origin and basic characteristics of each species are the product of intelligent purposeful design.
- That living and extinct species of organisms exist in groups or "kinds" which have always been separate from each other.
- That variation is limited within the boundaries of the created kinds.

4. Both of these opposed ways of looking at the world are assumptions or beliefs. Neither can be proved conclusively by science to be either right or wrong. They are faith propositions grounded in two mutually contradictory philosophical views of the world. . . .

THE GOAL OF CREATION SCIENTISTS

Our goal is not to bring a study of the Bible or the reading of the Genesis record of creation into the science classroom. Rather, if evolution or any other theory of origins is to be taught in a science class or textbook, it should be dealt with in a scientific manner. This means that dogmatism, protectionism and exclusivism should be excluded. Our goal is not to give Christians or the Christian world view a place of special advantage or monopoly control in the public schools, since this would be considered unconstitutional. Rather, if other belief systems are given a place, the biblical Christian alternatives should be placed in properly balanced competition with them.

We do not want to attack anybody else's religious faith in the science classroom, but we want an end to the use of science and science instruction falsely as a weapon against God and our Christian faith. Our goal is not that everybody in science and science education should be forced to think like a Christian. Rather, we want the system opened up again so that Christians can be free to think like Christians and function openly as Christians in science, education, scholarship, and other life callings without discrimination or prejudice because of their faith.

We want all citizens to be judged in society on the basis of their performance, not on the basis of whether or not they are willing to give in to what the majority believes or disbelieves. Under these conditions Christians, as well as those of other beliefs, will be better able to demonstrate the validity and value of their faith by the quality of their lives and accomplishments. Christians can give glory to God who has made it all possible.

THE CONSTITUTIONAL RIGHTS OF CHRISTIAN STUDENTS

The First Amendment to the U.S. Constitution states: "Congress shall make no law respecting an establishment of religion [i.e., a government sponsored church or religious belief system], *or prohibiting the free exercise thereof.* . . ." We have emphasized the Free Exercise Clause. This clause means, among other things, that the government may not offend any citizen by telling him that his religious belief is false and that he should believe in some other belief mandated by the government. Thus, when the State's schools teach a student who believes in creation by God, that evolution is a fact, even though it cannot be proved to be a fact, the State is telling the student that his or her religious belief is a falsehood. The State is illegally offending the believing student by violating that student's Free Exercise rights under the First Amendment.

EVOLUTION IS SPECULATIVE SCIENCE

A persistent criticism of science instruction is that evolution is often taught as "dogma" or as a "just so story." Mere scenarios of major evolutionary transformations are often presented as though they were "historical" observations, when neither the events nor their mechanism is actually known or perhaps even knowable. While some teachers do emphasize the theoretical nature of evolution, rarely is a critical view taken of this highly speculative field of science. As a result, the student and even the teacher are often led to conclude that there is no substantive criticism of evolutionary ideas among professional scientists, but such is hardly the case.

David N. Menton, *Teaching Origins in Public Schools*, 1991.

When the State protects evolutionary interpretations and theories from intelligent criticism, the State is making a religious

161

(or irreligious) dogma of evolution and again is violating the Free Exercise rights of the student who believes in creation.

When the State exclusively teaches materialistic theories and speculations concerning origins, without allowing for competition with alternative interpretations of the observed data, the State is teaching that a materialistic view of the universe is the only scientifically and intellectually respectable one. This constitutes a distortion of science that falsely makes science a weapon against religious faith. This violates the constitutional rights of Christian students.

Let's get the religious (or irreligious) indoctrination out of public school science and other subject areas by stopping the present policy of teaching evolutionary ideas dogmatically as fact and protecting them from criticism and competition. Let's stop the public schools from promoting atheism by teaching as science the belief that everything in the universe is the product of accident and that there is no Creator who created anything. Let's stop the public schools from promoting immorality by indoctrinating students in the belief that they are chance cousins of apes and therefore are no more subject to God's Moral Law than are the apes.

| "When you teach creation science, you're giving legitimacy to very bad scholarship."

CREATIONISM SHOULD NOT BE INCLUDED IN SCIENCE CURRICULA

Eugenie Scott, interviewed by Leon Lynn

In the following viewpoint, Eugenie Scott contends that creationism—a religious view of biological origins—should not be included in science curricula. Creation science research is rife with errors and inaccuracies, she points out; and, unlike serious scientists, creationists reject new information that could modify their theories. Evolutionary theory, however, is supported by ample evidence and helps to illustrate the scientific method. It is a primary theory of biology that all students should learn, she concludes. Scott holds a doctorate in physical anthropology and is executive director of the National Center for Science Education. She is interviewed by Leon Lynn, an education writer living in Milwaukee, Wisconsin.

As you read, consider the following questions:

1. In Scott's view, what is wrong with the argument that students should learn both evolution and creationism?
2. How are students who are not exposed to evolution placed at a disadvantage, according to the author?
3. In Scott's opinion, what should teachers do when they face pressure to stop teaching evolution?

Reprinted from Leon Lynn, "What's a Teacher to Do?" an interview with Eugenie Scott, *Rethinking Schools*, Winter 1997–98, vol. 12, no. 3, by permission of *Rethinking Schools*.

eon Lynn: *How likely is it that a science teacher in this country will encounter creationism, or feel pressure for teaching evolution?*

Eugenie Scott: At some time or another in their career, very likely. It varies based on where they work, of course. Usually, teachers in big cities will fare better than teachers in small towns and suburbs. But it's a common thing, and it seems to be getting more common.

There are two sides to this. One is the effort by creationists to teach some kind of religiously based idea as part of the science curriculum. That's usually pretty blatant. But there's another side, which can be a lot harder to see. Teachers get the message, sometimes overtly, sometimes more subtly, that evolution has become a controversial subject in their community and they'll just quietly stop teaching it, and evolution will sink out of the curriculum.

FLAWS OF THE "EQUAL-TIME" ARGUMENT

How do you respond when someone suggests that the fair thing to do is teach children about both evolution and creationism, and let them decide what to believe?

At its heart, the "equal-time" argument is substantially flawed. People who advocate it are basically saying we should teach that evolutionary theory—the idea that the universe changed through time, that the present is different from past—is equal in weight to the idea that the whole universe came into being at one time and hasn't changed since then. You can't do that in a science class. You can only deal with scientific evidence. There is copious evidence to support that evolution has occurred, and no evidence that everything was created at once and hasn't changed. Why would we pretend that an idea that was created outside of science is science? That's not fair.

It's perfectly reasonable to expose children to religious views of origin, but it's not OK to advocate those views as empirical truth. And the place for those ideas is not in the science curriculum.

Do you think students are harmed by exposure to creationism in their science class?

Yes. To begin with, these so-called alternatives to evolution are disadvantageous because they are simply factually wrong. Creation science literature is riddled with inaccuracies, misstatements. Students who learn it learn a lot of flat-out erroneous stuff. They also aren't learning the scientific method. The people pushing creation science aren't interested in modifying or revisiting their theories based on any new evidence, which is the basic premise of science. So when you teach creation science, you're giving legitimacy to very bad scholarship.

It's also a problem for students because if they don't learn evolution, they will be at a disadvantage when they take standardized tests. That includes college admissions tests. Evolution is not controversial at the college level. Scientists who work and teach at that level constantly tell me how amazed they are at the ignorance of students about evolution.

PRESSURE AGAINST TEACHING EVOLUTION

When teachers feel pressure to stop teaching evolution, what should they do?

To begin with, it's important to deal with people's feelings. If a religious parent is raising a complaint, for example, it's very important to make that parent realize you're not trying to change or challenge the child's religious faith. You need to say, "We are presenting the best scientific information, we want your children to learn it, but it's up to you and them whether they accept it or not." That often assuages parents' concern, because they're really afraid that when evolution is being taught, anti-religious ideas are being rammed down their children's throats.

Also, teachers need to support each other. If there are teachers in your school who are nervous about teaching evolution, others need to support them. Those teachers need to know they're not alone in case any flak comes along.

And probably the most important thing for teachers to do is to get administrative support. That is, if they can.

WHAT IS EVOLUTION?

Simply put, evolution is the scientific theory that all life forms on earth today are descended from a single cell, or at most a very few different cells. The diversity we see among species is the result of biological changes that have taken place over many hundreds of millions of years. During that time, new variations of plants and animals have appeared, through what the National Association of Biology Teachers terms "an unsupervised, impersonal, unpredictable, and natural process of temporal descent. . . ." Those new variations best able to adapt—to find food, escape predators, protect living space, or produce offspring—survived to pass along their traits to future generations. This is the process that Charles Darwin termed "natural selection" in his seminal 1859 work, *On the Origin of Species by Means of Natural Selection.*

Leon Lynn, *Rethinking Schools*, Winter 1997/1998.

What do you mean?

I've heard some great stories of administrators marching into the classroom and saying, "You will teach evolution, you signed a contract to teach the curriculum and that's part of it." I'd sure like to clone them, though, because we sure don't have many like that. I've been rather disappointed on the whole with the response of principals. The proper response in a situation like that is to explain to the parent the importance of evolution in the school curriculum. Instead, too many principals tend to appease the parent by talking to the teacher, and directing the teacher to "just skip it (evolution) this year." I've had teachers tell me stories like that at every conference I've ever attended.

Administrators are simply not doing their jobs on this. If a parent came in and said, "I don't want my child learning that the South lost the civil war," the principal would say, "Thanks for your input, but we have to teach the curriculum, including the part that says the North won." Or if you had a parent who was a Holocaust revisionist, you wouldn't see many principals telling teachers to stop teaching that the Holocaust took place. But they're willing to compromise the integrity of science and tell the teachers to downplay or skip evolution.

EVOLUTION IS NOT ANTI-GOD

Why is evolution treated differently?

The difference is partly due to people not wanting to be critical of religion. Administrators don't want to be labeled as being "anti-God." Remember, there are a lot of people who think that when you accept evolution, you have to reject religion. That's not true, but there are an awful lot of administrators who would rather just avoid the whole issue than start a debate like that with parents.

Another part of it is that there's a lot of ignorance among administrators about the central importance of evolution to science teaching. They don't realize that evolution is a central, unifying theory of biology, and that depriving students of learning it is a serious problem.

PERIODICAL BIBLIOGRAPHY

The following articles have been selected to supplement the diverse views presented in this chapter. Addresses are provided for periodicals not indexed in the *Readers' Guide to Periodical Literature*, the *Alternative Press Index*, the *Social Sciences Index*, or the *Index to Legal Periodicals and Books*.

Eric Buehrer and Edd Doerr — "Symposium: Should Public Schools Celebrate Thanksgiving and Christmas Holidays?" *Insight*, December 2, 1996. Available from 3600 New York Ave. NE, Washington, DC 20002.

Michael J. Gerson — "Public Schools Teach Bible as History," *U.S. News & World Report*, January 12, 1998.

Sarah Glazer — "Teaching Values," *CQ Researcher*, June 21, 1996. Available from 1414 22nd St. NW, Washington, DC 20037.

Kathleen Horan — "Pray in School? Pray to Whom?" *New York Times*, September 9, 1995.

Thomas Lickona — "The Case for Character Education," *Tikkun*, January/February 1997.

Leon Lynn — "The Evolution of Creationism," *Rethinking Schools*, Winter 1997–1998.

David Masci — "Evolution vs. Creationism," *CQ Researcher*, August 22, 1997.

John B. Massen — "Thinking 'About' Religion: The Need for Freethought in the Curriculum," *Free Inquiry*, Spring 1996. Available from PO Box 664, Amherst, NY 14226-0664.

Barbara McEwan — "Public Schools, Religion, and Public Responsibility," *USA Today*, May 1997.

Madalyn O'Hair — "The Matter of Prayer," *American Atheist*, August 1995.

Robert L. Simmonds — "Common Ground with the Religious Right," *Education Digest*, January 1997.

Sheldon Vanauken — "The Supreme Court and Young Minds," *Crisis*, January 1996. Available from PO Box 10559, Riverton, NJ 08076-0559.

David Van Biema — "Spiriting Prayer into School," *Time*, April 27, 1998.

CHAPTER 5

How Could Public Education Be Improved?

Chapter Preface

In 1983, Education Secretary Terrel H. Bell published *A Nation at Risk*, a report concluding that U.S. students' academic skills were far behind those of students in other industrialized countries. High school seniors were so far behind, the report claimed, that a relatively high number of them—at least 10 percent—were functionally illiterate or lacked basic math skills.

In response to this report, many educators initially supported the push for national educational standards in the early 1990s. As part of a list of educational goals intended to be met by the year 2000, policymakers backed the creation of standards in thirteen subject areas. These standards, which would be compiled by groups of professional educators, were to explicitly state what academic skills and knowledge students should have after completing grades four, eight, and twelve. Under the 1994 Goals 2000 law, states would be given federal money to implement reform measures to get students to meet these national standards.

Support for national educational standards waned, however, after the 1994 release of the proposed history standards, which many historians claimed were unscholarly and "too politically correct." These standards were rejected by the Senate and revised in 1996. Then in March 1996, the proposed national standards for English were denounced for being unclear. Policymakers and concerned citizens began to question the decision to approve national standards at all, and many states chose not to accept federal money for the Goals 2000 initiative.

Advocates for national standards contend that creating specific requirements for student achievement is necessary if the U.S. wishes to compete in the global economy with an educated workforce. Some conservative critics, however, maintain that the use of national standards takes control away from local school boards. Todd Tiahrt, Republican representative from Kansas, argues that "we need to . . . demand stronger academic basics at the local level. . . . Another Washington-knows-best solution is no solution at all." Liberal opponents, moreover, assert that the issue of unequal funding of schools must be addressed before standards can be set. "Any policy to establish benchmarks for achievement without creating equity in the educational resources available to children would be a cruel hoax," reads a statement signed by several critics of the National Council on Education Standards and Testing.

The authors in the following chapter debate several additional ideas and proposals for improving public education.

> "The only practical way to achieve liberalism's aim of greater social justice is to pursue conservative educational policies."

CONSERVATIVE EDUCATIONAL POLICIES WOULD BENEFIT PUBLIC SCHOOLS

E.D. Hirsch Jr.

E.D. Hirsch Jr. is a professor of education and humanities at the University of Virginia in Charlottesville. He is also the author of *Cultural Literacy* and *The Schools We Need and Why We Don't Have Them.* In the following viewpoint, Hirsch argues that public schools should be guided by conservative educational policies that emphasize traditional instructional methods such as phonics, fact memorization, and knowledge-based learning. Liberal educational policies that de-emphasize the need for basic skills, rigor, and challenging subject matter lead to a decline in academic achievement and an increase in educational inequities, Hirsch contends.

As you read, consider the following questions:

1. According to Hirsch, how do the educational theories of Antonio Gramsci and Paulo Freire differ?
2. Why is "individualized instruction" often ineffective, in the author's opinion?
3. Who has been hurt the most by progressive educational policies, in Hirsch's opinion?

Reprinted from E.D. Hirsch Jr., "Why Traditional Education Is More Progressive," *The American Enterprise*, March/April 1997, by permission of *The American Enterprise*, a Washington, D.C.–based magazine of politics, business, and culture.

I would label myself a political liberal and an educational conservative, or perhaps more accurately, an educational pragmatist. Political liberals really ought to oppose progressive educational ideas because they have led to practical failure and greater social inequity. The only practical way to achieve liberalism's aim of greater social justice is to pursue conservative educational policies.

ANTONIO GRAMSCI AND PAULO FREIRE

This is not a new idea. In 1932, the Communist intellectual Antonio Gramsci detected the paradoxical consequences of the new "democratic" education that stressed naturalistic approaches over hard work and the transmission of knowledge. Writing from jail (where he had been imprisoned by Mussolini) Gramsci observed that:

> Previously pupils at least acquired a certain baggage of concrete facts. Now there will no longer be any baggage to put in order.
> . . . The most paradoxical aspect of it all is that this new type of school is advocated as being democratic, while in fact it is destined not merely to perpetuate social differences but to crystallize them in Chinese complexities.

Gramsci saw that it was a serious error to discredit learning methods like phonics and memorization of the multiplication table as "outdated" or "conservative." That was the nub of the standoff between himself and another prominent educational theorist of the political Left, Paulo Freire. Like Gramsci, Freire (a Brazilian) was interested in methods of educating the poor. Unlike Gramsci, Freire has been quite influential in the United States.

Like other educational progressives, Freire rejected traditional subject matter and derided the "banking theory of schooling," whereby the teacher provides the child with a lot of "rote-learned" information. This conservative approach, according to Freire, numbs the critical faculties of students and preserves the oppressor class. He called for a change of both content and methods. Teachers should present new content that would celebrate the culture of the oppressed, and they should also instruct in new methods that would encourage intellectual resistance. In short, Freire, like other modern educational writers, linked political and educational progressivism.

Gramsci took the opposite view. He held that political progressivism demanded educational traditionalism. The oppressed class should be taught to master the tools of power and authority—the ability to read, write, and communicate—and should gain enough traditional knowledge to understand the worlds of nature and culture surrounding them. Children, particularly the children of the poor, should not be encouraged to follow "natural" inclinations, which would only keep them ignorant and make them slaves of emotion. They should learn the value of hard work, gain the knowledge that leads to understanding, and master the traditional culture in order to command its rhetoric, as Gramsci himself had learned to do.

THE PROBLEM WITH EDUCATIONAL LIBERALISM

History has proved Gramsci a better prophet than Freire. Modern nations that have followed Gramscian principles have improved the condition and heightened the political, social, and economic power of their lower classes. By contrast, nations that have adopted the principles of Freire (including our own) have failed to elevate the economic and social status of their most underprivileged citizens.

Gramsci was not the only observer to predict the inegalitarian consequences of the educational methods variously described as "naturalistic," "project-oriented," "critical-thinking," and "democratic." I focus on Gramsci as a revered theorist of the Left in order to make a strategic point. Ideological polarizations on educational issues tend to be facile and premature. Not only is there a practical separation between educational conservatism and political conservatism, but there is an inverse relation between educational liberalism and social liberalism. Educational liberalism is a sure means for preserving the social status quo, whereas the best practices of educational conservatism are the only means whereby children from disadvantaged homes can secure the knowledge and skills that will enable them to improve their condition.

Unfortunately, many of today's American educators paint traditional education as the arch-enemy of "humane" modern education. Even everyday classroom language unfairly pits the two alternatives against one another. Here are some typical descriptions used by progressives to compare old and new methods:

- Traditional vs. Modern
- Merely verbal vs. Hands-on
- Premature vs. Developmentally appropriate
- Fragmented vs. Integrated
- Boring vs. Interesting
- Lockstep vs. Individualized

Parents presented with such choices for their children's education would be unlikely to prefer traditional, merely verbal, premature, fragmented, boring, and lockstep instruction to instruction that is modern, hands-on, developmentally appropriate, integrated, interesting, and individualized. But of course this is a loaded and misleading contrast. Let's look at those simple polarities one at a time.

FAULTY PROGRESSIVIST ARGUMENTS

• *Traditional vs. Modern Instruction.* Reproduced below is a typical progressivist caricature of traditional knowledge-based education:

> The emphasis that permeated the traditional school was recitation, memorization, recall, testing, grades, promotion, and failure. And for this kind of education it was necessary that children primarily listen, sit quiet and attentive in seats, try to fix in their minds what the teacher told them, commit to memory the lessons assigned to them, and then, somewhat like a cormorant, be ready at all times to disgorge the intake. . . . This fixed, closed, authoritarian system of education perfectly fitted the needs of a static religion, a static church, a static caste system, a static economic system.

This argument ignores the fact that traditional knowledge-based schooling is currently employed with great success in most other advanced nations. It fails to note that challenging subject matter—the core of traditional education—can be taught in a lively, demanding way.

If parents were told straightforwardly that the so-called "untraditional" or "modern" mode of education now dominant in our schools has coincided with the decline of academic competencies among our students, they might be less enthusiastic about the experiment. When these dismal outcomes are pointed out, progressive educators usually reply that progressivism has never been tried "properly." That is false. It is merely the fail-safe defense that apologists use for all unsuccessful theories.

• *Merely Verbal vs. Hands-on Instruction.* The idea that students will learn better if they see, feel, and touch the subjects they are studying has such obvious merit that it would be amazing if traditional education did not make use of multisensory methods of teaching. And indeed, if one studies the history of educational methods, one finds that every traditionalist theorist advocates hands-on methods where they lead to good results. The hidden progressivist agenda on this issue lies in the disparagement of verbal learning. An essential aspect of understanding in human beings is the ability to speak or write about what one has assimilated. Disparaging verbal learning is especially harmful to children who come to school with restricted vocabularies because of family disadvantages.

• *Premature vs. Developmentally Appropriate Instruction.* A fear of "premature" instruction has led to the removal of significant knowledge from grade-school curricula. Once again, the primary victims of this impoverishment of education are disadvantaged children. Advantaged children gain much of the withheld knowledge at home. If "premature" instruction is such a grave risk, why do young children of comparable ages in other lands absorb such knowledge with great benefit and no ill effects? The label "developmentally appropriate" is generally applied without any empirical basis—simply on the basis of a "gut reaction" by progressive educators.

OTHER FALSE POLARITIES

• *Fragmented vs. Integrated Instruction.* Both traditionalists and progressives prefer instruction which shows how things fit together and at the same time helps secure what is being learned by reinforcing it in a variety of contexts. The pseudopolarization over "fragmented" teaching has been exploited ever since the early twentieth century to disparage the direct teaching of subject matters such as mathematics, spelling, and biology in classes that are specifically devoted to those topics. The whole outdated concept of subject matters is to be replaced by "thematic" or "project-oriented" instruction. The result has been not integration at all but the failure of students to learn the most basic elements of the different subject matters.

• *Boring vs. Interesting Instruction.* This opposition is used to withhold academic subject matters such as ancient history and science from children in the early grades on the grounds that true education proceeds from the child's own experience rather than externally "imposed" concepts. Because it is true that children learn best when new knowledge builds upon what they already know, progressives insist that early schooling should be limited to subjects that have direct relevance to the child's life, such as "my neighborhood" and similar "relevant" topics.

Yet every person with enough schooling to be reading these words knows that subject matters by themselves do not repel or attract interest. An effective teacher can make the most distant subject interesting, and an ineffective one can make any subject dull. The presumption that the affairs of one's own community are more interesting than those of faraway times or places is contradicted in every classroom that studies dinosaurs and fairy tales. Progressives' warnings about classic subject matter being "boring" or "irrelevant" simply conceal an anti-intellectual, anti-academic bias.

• *Lockstep vs. Individualized Instruction*. Traditional instruction is said to impose the same content on every student, without taking into account the child's individual strengths, weaknesses, and interests, whereas modern instruction is tailored to each child's individual temperament. Unquestionably, one-on-one tutorials are the most effective mode of teaching. How, then, can we explain the paradox that individuals learn more and better in schools where greater emphasis is placed on whole-class instruction than on individualized tutoring? How do we explain the research finding that even students needing extra help make more progress when whole class instruction is emphasized over individual tutorials?

BACK TO BASICS LEARNING

The "core knowledge" theory, which some call "back to basics" learning, involves giving students specific sets of facts—a core body of knowledge that they must master. Specific concepts are taught to students, with an emphasis on memorization.

A chief proponent of that method is E.D. Hirsch, author of the best-selling book *Cultural Literacy*. Backers of core knowledge argue that students must have a firm grasp of important concepts and facts, such as the names of presidents and the dates of major historical events. In 1995, Virginia's state Board of Education implemented standards for the social sciences based on the core knowledge theory. The standards won an endorsement from the American Federation of Teachers (AFT), one of the nation's largest teachers' unions, and have been examined by 11 other states.

Issues and Controversies On File, June 27, 1997.

The answer lies in simple arithmetic. It is impossible to provide effective one-on-one tutorials to 25 students at a time. When one student is being coached individually, 24 others are being left to their own devices, usually in silent seatwork. When, on the other hand, knowledge is effectively given to the entire group simultaneously, more students are learning much more of the time. The occasional individual help they receive is all the more effective. By contrast, classrooms that march under the banner of individual attention are often characterized by individual neglect.

THE CONSEQUENCES OF PROGRESSIVE EDUCATION

In short, many progressive educational assertions that have attained the status of unquestioned fact by being repeated constantly are huge oversimplifications. They wither under close scrutiny. And they have done serious harm.

Among other results, hostility to traditional schooling methods and subjects has fostered inequality. The record is clear. In the period from 1942 to 1966—before progressive theories had spread throughout our schools—public education had begun to close the economic gap between races and social classes. But after 1966, as SAT scores went into steep decline, the black-white wage gap abruptly stopped shrinking.

Black Americans currently earn about 16 percent less than whites at the same grade level. Social scientists studying this have recently shown that 12 out of those 16 percentage points can be explained by the fact that blacks have been less well schooled. When black and white earners are matched by their actual educational attainment, rather than just the grade level they achieved, the black-white wage disparity drops to less than 5 percent, and some of this remainder can be explained by factors other than racial discrimination.

It is poor children who have been hurt most by the dominance of "progressive" ideas, but they are not the only victims. Almost all American children have been receiving inferior schooling that hinders them from developing their capacities to the fullest. Compared to the rigorous educations received by many Europeans and Asians, most American children are "underprivileged."

KNOWLEDGE-BASED EDUCATION

Is there an available alternative to today's failed progressive education? Yes. That alternative is knowledge-based education.

I presented suggestions for knowledge-based education in my 1987 book *Cultural Literacy*. Since then, thanks to some very independent-minded principals and teachers, I have gained valuable direct experience with teaching challenging subject matter in early grades. In 1990, Dr. Constance Jones, the principal of Three Oaks Elementary School in Fort Myers, Florida, made her large, mixed-population public school the first in the nation to follow the principles of *Cultural Literacy*. The stunning success of Three Oaks then led another principal, Mr. Jeffrey Litt, to introduce the same principles to his school, the Mohegan School, No. 67, located in the South Bronx. The Fort Myers experiment received a lot of attention, but it was the remarkable early results achieved in the South Bronx that drew the attention of network news programs, *Reader's Digest*, and other magazines and newspapers. Public notice for both schools led other elementary schools to make the arduous shift to a solid, knowledge-based curriculum. The education press now calls our school reform effort the Core Knowledge Movement. It has been fully adopted in more than 350 public schools in 40 states, and a much larger number of schools are successfully using the foundation's principles and materials.

The fact that so many energetic principals and teachers have been willing and even eager to break out of "progressive" education and return to more effective traditional methods is our best hope for America's educational future.

| "Since kids have this huge range of different needs, different interests and different ways of learning, we've got to have a wide diversity of schools."

PROGRESSIVE EDUCATIONAL POLICIES WOULD BENEFIT PUBLIC SCHOOLS

Deborah Meier

The creation of progressive, self-governing learning communities can lead to true educational reform, argues Deborah Meier in the following viewpoint. Instead of drafting national academic standards and implementing impersonal, one-size-fits-all teaching methods, parents, teachers, and communities should work together to design small new schools that address students' needs and interests, she contends. These schools would emphasize respect for parents, teachers, and children, personalized instruction, active learning, and the development of the capacity for astute, probing thought. Meier, former codirector of the Central Park East Secondary School in New York City, is program director at Mission Hill Elementary School in Roxbury, Massachusetts.

As you read, consider the following questions:

1. In Meier's opinion, what is flawed about the standards-driven educational reform movement?
2. What is the kindergarten model of education, according to the author?
3. In Meier's view, what are the types of questions a well-educated person asks about the world?

Excerpted from chapter 6 of Deborah Meier, *Transforming Public Education* (New York: Teachers College Press), ©1997 by Teachers College, Columbia University. All rights reserved. Reprinted by permission of the publisher.

W e stand poised between alternate ways of imagining schools of tomorrow. The tough part is that to some ex tent each of these ways is often espoused by some of the same people, and teachers and citizens alike are led to believe that they can both be carried out simultaneously. Or people try to weave in and out of each, with the result that they end up never decisively setting course.

The two that interest me most are, not surprisingly, often seen as close cousins. This is due to the fact that they are both espoused by people who come out of a similar tradition—progressive and liberal-minded. The kinds of schools they'd both probably like to see are, indeed, in some ways quite similar, with a focus on critical inquiry, curriculum depth, and collaboration and a downplaying of multiple-choice testing, rote memorization, and highly competitive classrooms.

What they disagree about is how to get there, and as a corollary to this, what must be sacrificed for "later" in order to get there "sooner." Faced with what may be a more imminent danger from the far right, it is tempting to forget these differences. But that would be a mistake because, in fact and despite their often complementary intentions, these two ways stand in chilling contrast to each other.

THE STANDARDS-DRIVEN REFORM MOVEMENT

One way, the position of the supporters of Goals 2000 and, indeed, the entire standards-driven reform movement, rests on the assumption that top-down support for bottom-up change— which both positions are rhetorically for—means that the top will do the critical intellectual work of defining purposes and content as well as how to measure them, while the bottom does the "nuts and bolts," the "how-to"—a sort of "men's work" versus "women's work" division of labor. [Goals 2000 is a government-supported plan, initiated in the early 1990s, to create national academic standards and improve student achievement by the year 2000.] This approach seeks a consensus of academic expertise and mainstream political correctness, reinforced by high-stakes testing to discipline unruly kids, teachers, and local school boards. (While it now tends toward a liberal/mainstream consensus, it's worth noting that it's an approach that could just as easily tilt toward a very different, radically right-wing political consensus.)

The Goals 2000 agenda and the state-mandated versions that are flowing from it, with their focus on measurable goals and standards and their vision set by international competition and the emerging global economy, are weighted down with the assumption that the task of school reform is far too important to leave the critical intellectual work to those responsible for implementing school practice. While much of the work emanating from the standard-setters is worthy, it cannot lead either to high-level intellectual work in our classrooms or to solving our global economic crisis.

ANOTHER WAY

There is another possible set of assumptions, based on a different vision of human capacity. This way of thinking leads to rejecting top-down reforms unless they are useful to the creation and sustenance of self-governing learning communities responsible for collaboratively and publicly deciding really important issues. The kind of education we want for our young requires schools that see themselves as membership communities, not service organizations. In such communities ideas are discussed, purposes argued about, and judgment exercised by parents, teachers, and students because that is at the heart of what it means to be well educated: having one's own wonderful ideas. Students can't learn, nor can the adults who must show them the way, unless they can practice what they preach.

At the moment, many political conservatives are also arguing against the creation of a national, standards-driven system. The trouble is not only that the political Right may support some rather horrendous locally driven standards, but also that they are also focused on eliminating the whole problem by abolishing public responsibility for all children's education. They seek, in fact, the elimination of a public system of schooling and its replacement by a free market of private schools. Thus, while the opposition to the imposing of national standards is alive and well these days, those in opposition are not all of one mind. It would be unwise, however, to drop the argument just because of the sometimes unlikely alliances it has created. In fact, some of those who are attracted to the Right's anti-federalist cause are motivated by many of the same concerns I have.

I've been told, during the past few years, that I'm ignoring the train that's already left the station and is coming down the line, the "do-it-or-else" express. This new wave of the future, it is suggested, is not dependent on any central congressional bodies. (The power of the SATs . . . , for example, is not derived from any legislative act.) But if history is any guide, the kind of fast-track solutions being proposed will often turn out to be expensive dead ends. Designed in heady conference centers, the blueprints are usually too unwieldy, covering everything but the kitchen sink, a patched-together consensus that satisfies no one, and finally just too susceptible to local resistance to produce what their architects had in mind.

One imagines a countermandate to the "all students will" dictums being invented by expert, university-based task forces: for example, how about insisting that standards be phased in only as fast as the school can bring its adult staff up to the standards it expects of all 18-year-olds? That might delay the train just a little.

A Progressive Alternative

We in New York have historically lived under the imposition of an awesome array of local and state curricular mandates and outcomes assessments. (Except for private schools, which were always free to ignore them and always have.) Every so often someone gets the idea to create still a new set, generally laid right on top of the old one, and then moves on to other things. New York teachers are experienced and inventive saboteurs of the best and worst of such plans. We are home, therefore, to some of the greatest as well as some of the worst of schools.

But an alternative to the Goals 2000 approach that rests squarely on a strong system of public schooling and a commitment to democracy is gathering surprising national momentum. The movement to empower teachers with the capacity to make professional judgments and the creation of small schools in which parents, teachers, and community can work closely together are two of the promising developments that may undermine the top-down plans.

We also have some hard-headed real history of school reform to point to, on a scale that should make it hard to dismiss this "other" way as suitable only for the brave and foolish, the maverick, and the exceptional. It's no longer "alternative," but almost mainstream.

When a handful of like-minded teachers in East Harlem's Community School District Four started a "progressive," "open education" elementary school—Central Park East—in 1974, we were encouraged by the then district superintendent, Anthony Alvarado, to pay little heed to rules and regulations. We were told to create the kind of school we believed would work for the children of District Four. This revolutionary autonomy, referred to locally as "creative compliance" or "creative noncompliance," was simply doing publicly and collaboratively what many of us had long done behind closed doors.

Central Park East (CPE), along with more than 30 other small schools of choice begun by District Four over the next 10 years, was and remains an amazing success story. We lived a somewhat lonely existence for a decade, but today both the CPE schools and the District Four "way" have been roughly replicated in dozens of New York City school districts and are now part of accepted citywide reform plans. What they share is a way of looking at children reminiscent of good kindergarten practice. Put another way, they are based on what we know about how human beings learn as well as a deep-seated respect for all of the parties involved—parents, teachers, and kids.

THE KINDERGARTEN MODEL

Kindergarten is the one place—for many children maybe the last place—where such mutual respect has been a traditional norm (even if not always practiced). A kindergarten teacher, for example, is expected to know children well, even if they don't hand in their homework, finish their Friday tests, or pay attention. Kindergarten teachers know that learning must be personalized, just because kids come that way—no two alike. They know that parents and the community must be partners, or kids will be shortchanged. Kindergarten teachers know that helping children learn to become more self-reliant is part of their job definition—starting with tying shoes and going to the bathroom on their own.

Alas, it is the last time children are given such independence, encouraged to make choices, and allowed to move about on their own. Having learned to use the bathroom by themselves at age five, at age six they are then required to wait until the whole class lines up at bathroom time. In kindergarten, parent and teacher meet to talk and often have each other's phone numbers. After that it's mainly a checklist of numbers and letters. The older they get, the less we take into account the importance of their own interests, their own active learning.

In kindergarten we design our rooms for real work, not just passive listening. We put things in the room that we have reason to believe will appeal to children, grab their interests, and engage their minds and hearts. Teachers in kindergarten are editors, critics, cheerleaders, and caretakers, not just lecturers or deliverers of instruction. What education reformer Ted Sizer calls "coaching" is second nature to the kindergarten teacher, who takes for granted that her job description includes curriculum as well as natural ongoing assessment. What's true for students is true for teachers: they have less and less authority, responsibility, and independence as their charges get older. Until, of course, they make it into an elite college or graduate school. Then both teachers and students go back into kindergarten.

Indeed, it was Ted Sizer who, when he came to visit our school, pointed out to us that the kindergarten principles of Central Park East were the same principles he was espousing for the nation's high schools. So we made the decision to see if we could use the principles of a good kindergarten as the basis for running a good high school. We opened Central Park East Secondary School in 1985 with a seventh grade and grew one grade each year thereafter.

PROGRESSIVE EDUCATIONAL STANDARDS

At Central Park East Secondary School in New York City, . . . standards for learning and student work have been established by the school's faculty and continuously evolve. Each student had to define clear individual goals that also meet the general learning standards. The result is "standards without standardization." The school also encourages active learning, group work, and engagement with the outside world, as it strives to meet the individual needs of each student. . . .

Graduation at Central Park East involves completing work across the curriculum as shown in portfolios that are evaluated by teams of teachers, students, outside experts, and community members. Portfolio information is shared with parents, and classroom-based assessment information feeds into the school's self-evaluation and outside reviews.

Monty Neill, *Rethinking Schools*, Summer 1996.

One thing we very much wanted was to break away from the contemporary mode of breaking everything down into discrete bits and pieces—whether subject matter or "thinking skills." We were determined to keep the elementary school tradition of respect for the wholeness of both subject matter and human learning intact.

Another priority for us was creating a setting in which all members of the community were expected to engage in the discussion of ideas and in the "having of [their own] wonderful ideas," as teacher and author Eleanor Duckworth has put it. Indeed, one of our most prominently stated, upfront aims was the cultivation of what we came to call "habits of mind," habits that apply to all academic and nonacademic subject matter and to all thoughtful human activities.

The five habits we came up with are not exhaustive, but they suggest the kind of questions that we believed a well-educated person raises about his world:

1. How do we know what we think we know? What's our evidence? How credible is it?
2. Whose viewpoint are we hearing, reading, seeing? What other viewpoints might there be if we changed our position?
3. How is one thing connected to another? Is there a pattern here?
4. How else might it have been? What if? Supposing that?
5. What difference does it make? Who cares?

NO 'ONE BEST WAY'

Proud as we are of these schools, we do not see what we do as the "one best or only way" to educate children. As Seymour Fliegel, a former deputy superintendent in Community District Four, has put it:

> The aim here has been to create a system that—instead of trying to fit all students into some standardized school—has a school to fit every student in this district. No kid gets left out, no kid gets lost. Every kid is important, every kid can learn if you put him or her in the right environment. But since kids have this huge range of different needs, different interests and different ways of learning, we've got to have a wide diversity of schools.

While it has taken time for the District Four ideas to "catch on" or for Central Park East's particular approach to spread, today both are "in the mainstream." Everyone is imitating District Four's system of choices.

It was the creation of a broad and diverse set of new schools, not the reforming of existing schools, that was the crucial decision made in District Four's "revolution" of two decades ago. It meant the district could focus on encouraging school people, not monitoring them for compliance with district-mandated reforms. The next phase will do well not to ignore the lessons learned: It's easier to design a new school culture than to change an existing one. And it's the whole school culture, not this or that program, that stands in the way of learning.

The role of parents in the new schools, as mentioned earlier, is another central issue. Choice offered a way of providing for increased professional decision-making without pitting parents and teachers against each other in a useless power struggle. Furthermore, small schools of choice offered everyone vastly increased time to meet together and work out differences—teachers, teachers and families, and parents through their formal and informal structures. The time needed is considerable but definitely worth it. One top-down mandate we'd have no trouble with would be legislating that employers provide time off for parents to attend school meetings.

Ensuring 'Accountability'

What about the loud cries for "accountability" that play such a major role in support of top-down schemes? Who will tell us if it's "world-class"? How will we know for sure how students stack up against each other nationally and internationally in the great race to see who's first?

The capacity to create schools that are accountable to their own immediate community—parents, kids, and fellow staff members—is far easier in small, self-governed communities. However, the ways in which schools that set out to be independent and idiosyncratic can meet the legitimate needs for broader taxpayer accountability requires new thinking. We've built our current system of public accountability on the basis of the factory model school with its interchangeable parts. It's no wonder that we get almost no useful or honest information back.

The danger here is that we will cramp the needed innovations with over-ambitious accountability demands. Practical realism must prevail. Changes in the daily conduct of schooling—whether it's new curriculum or pedagogy or just new ways of collaborating and governing—are hard, slow, and above all immensely time-consuming; they require qualities of trust and patience that we are not accustomed to.

The structural reforms—changes in size, the role of choice, and shifts in power relationships—may be hard to make. To some degree these are the changes that can be "imposed" from above. The trouble is that they merely lay the ground for the slow and steady work that will impact on young people's intellectual and moral development. That's the tough realization. Some claim we can't afford such slow changes. They are wrong. There is nothing faster. If we go faster we may get somewhere faster—but not where we need to go.

Reforms and Democracy

Although the reasons for the current national concern about schooling may have little to do with democracy, the reforms described here have everything to do with it. Giving wider choices and more power to those who are closest to the classroom are not reforms that appeal to busy legislators, politicians, and central board officials. They seem too messy and too hard to track. They cannot be initiated on Monday and measured on Friday. They require fewer constraints and fewer rules—not more of them. They require asking why it matters and who cares, not lists of 465 skills, facts, and concepts multiplied by the number of disciplines academia can invent. They require initiating a debate in this nation that might shake us to the roots, a debate about what it is we value so dearly that we incarcerate our children for 12 years to make sure they've "got it."

A democratic society has a right to insist that the central function of schooling is to cultivate the mental and moral habits that a modern democracy requires. Such habits, in fact, can be troubling and uncomfortable to have, but, we hope, hard to shake. Openness to other viewpoints, the capacity to sustain uncertainty, the ability to act on partial knowledge, the inclination to step into the shoes of others—these are the controversial requirements, for example. Until we face such questions, it makes little sense to keep asking for better tools to measure what we haven't agreed about.

"What's it for?" the young ask often enough. It's time adults took the question seriously. There are no silver bullets when it comes to raising children right, no fast-track solutions with guaranteed cures. Just hard work, keeping your eyes on the prize, and lots of patience for the disagreements that inevitably arise.

"[An] investment in education is one we could easily afford right now."

INCREASED FUNDING WOULD IMPROVE PUBLIC EDUCATION

Jesse Jackson

In the following viewpoint, Jesse Jackson contends that more public money should be spent on education. Increased funding is needed to build, renovate, repair, and properly equip schools, he points out. Concerned citizens must insist that the government provide up-to-date facilities and premium learning environments for students regardless of their race or socioeconomic status. Jackson is president of the National Rainbow Coalition, a social justice organization. He has been active in civil rights issues since the 1960s.

As you read, consider the following questions:

1. According to Jackson, how much more money is spent on prison inmates than on public school students in Chicago?
2. What "unspoken message" do the students of DuSable High receive, in the author's opinion?
3. What would be the results of increased public spending on education, in Jackson's view?

Reprinted from Jesse Jackson, "New Schools Now," *Liberal Opinion Week*, March 23, 1998, by permission of the Los Angeles Times Syndicate. Copyright 1998 by the Los Angeles Times.

Neuqua Valley High School is the promised land. In this new $62 million school, every classroom has computers with Internet access, telephones and televisions. Students here know the community is offering them the best of learning environments.

Seventy percent of the voters in the suburban school district west of Chicago in which Neuqua Valley High is located approved the $97 million bond issue and property tax increase needed to build new schools in the area.

DuSable High in downtown Chicago doesn't compare.

Neuqua Valley, for instance, boasts an Olympic-sized "fast pool" deep enough for speed training. On a visit to 55-year-old DuSable, we found the pool closed because the roof over it had collapsed.

Parents of students at DuSable care deeply about education, but with 98 percent of them living near or below poverty level, there is a limit to what they can afford.

Cook County Alternative School

At Cook County Alternative School, conditions are even more primitive. The school, run by the public school system but located in the Cook County Jail, offers high school–level courses to its inmates. Ninety-six percent of its students are African American or Hispanic.

In math and reading tests, 11th graders at this school scored at levels set for seventh graders. Ironically, they scored a little better than the average for all Chicago public schools. When I asked them why, they said, "Focus. In here, we can focus." They don't have to worry about drive-by shootings. They get three meals a day and medical care. Chicago spends an average of $18,615 a year on each inmate, compared with an average of $6,941 on each public school student.

Separate and Unequal

Recently, the Rainbow/PUSH Action Network gathered 250 students, educators, judges and state legislators for an up-close look at these three high schools, which together provide a snapshot of the reality of American public education today: separate and unequal.

In the historic 1954 decision in *Brown vs. Board of Education*, the Supreme Court declared racial segregation in schools—exemplified by the South's claim of separate but equal facilities—unconstitutional. The court knew that racially separate schools in the South were never equal. White students got the new texts, the best facilities. Blacks received a second-class education.

Today, segregation by race is unconstitutional, but public education is increasingly separate and unequal, divided by class and race. The gulfs are far greater than those of the old South. Author Jonathan Kozol calls this the "savage inequality" of American education.

'EDUCATION IS THE ONLY WAY UP, KIDS'

©1993 Engelhardt in the *St. Louis Dispatch*. Reprinted with permission.

Children, Kozol notes, are very sensitive to the unspoken message. Children in the affluent suburbs may rebel, party too hard and study too little. But they know, when they arrive each morning at schools like Neuqua Valley High, that much is expected of them. Some may stray, but most will find their way.

Children at schools like DuSable High might have iron-willed parents who lecture them about the importance of education and the need to stay away from troublemakers. They may even receive support from ministers and encouragement from some gifted teachers. But each day, these students know that not much is expected from them. A few will overcome neglect and beat the odds. But many learn to forget their dreams and wind up dropping out or worse.

America's economy is strong. The rich are richer than ever. Wages have finally begun to rise across the board. In Washington, D.C., and in most states, legislators argue about surpluses, not deficits.

EVERY CHILD COUNTS

In the early years of the Republic, America led the world in providing public education. It was a statement of our democracy: Every child counts. It was also a statement of our faith: Every child is graced by God.

We could easily afford to reaffirm these beliefs. Just as President Eisenhower once orchestrated the creation of the interstate highway network, we could create a federal-state program to build and repair schools. In this way we could ensure that every child in America has the opportunity to attend a properly equipped school that encourages them to achieve their dreams.

Building more schools would no doubt be expensive. The General Accounting Office reports that it would take more than $100 billion simply to bring existing public schools up to safety codes. The green eyeshade crowd would mumble and grumble about increased public spending and foregone tax cuts. But this investment in education is one we could easily afford right now. We also could expect lavish returns: better-educated workers, young people steered away from crime, and the rewards of a stronger and more just democracy grounded in opportunity for every child.

Yet Washington isn't in the mood for historic initiatives. The White House is beset with problems. . . . And Congress seems content to pass the time renaming airports.

People of conscience must challenge this complacency. It took the civil rights movement to end segregation. It will require a similarly massive effort to eliminate the savage inequality in our schools.

> "More money and more teachers are nothing more than self-serving strategies to enhance the wealth and power of the education establishment."

INCREASED FUNDING DOES NOT IMPROVE PUBLIC EDUCATION

Walter Williams

Increased funding for schools does not improve public education, argues syndicated columnist Walter Williams in the following viewpoint. Ample evidence proves that higher expenditures per student, smaller class sizes, and above-average teacher salaries do not boost student performance. In fact, the author points out, states that spend less on public-school funding often have higher levels of student achievement. Society should focus on providing genuine solutions to the educational crisis, such as more charter schools, concludes Williams.

As you read, consider the following questions:

1. According to Williams, what are the per-student expenditures in Minnesota and Iowa?
2. What evidence proves that high teacher salaries do not result in increased student performance, in the author's opinion?
3. Why do charter schools appear to be one effective solution to the educational crisis, in Williams's opinion?

Reprinted from Walter Williams, "More Money, Better Education?" *Conservative Chronicle*, February 10, 1999, by permission of Walter Williams and Creators Syndicate.

President Bill Clinton is traipsing up and down the land, calling for more money for education. This time, it's money to hire 100,000 additional teachers in order to reduce class size and hopefully improve public education.

A just-released report by the American Legislative Exchange Council, "Report Card on American Education," suggests that taxpayers, parents and students are about to be had again.

THE "MORE-MONEY" SHAM

Let's examine the education establishment's more-money, better-education sham. New Jersey ranks No. 1 in the nation in terms of expenditures per student ($10,900). Washington, D.C., is a close second at $10,300. If educationists are right, New Jersey and Washington should have the highest level of student achievement in the land.

Think again. New Jersey ranks 29th in student achievement. As for Washington, the only thing preventing it from being dead last in student achievement is Mississippi.

Minnesota ranks first in the nation in terms of student achievement, and Iowa ranks second. If we accepted the more-money-better education sham, we'd think Minnesota and Iowa are really up there in per-student expenditures. Think again. Minnesota ranks 27th in expenditure per student ($6,300), and Iowa ranks a lowly 30th ($6,000). There is no relation between expenditures and student performance.

CLASS SIZE AND TEACHER SALARIES

You say: "Williams, you're forgetting about reducing the number of students per teacher. That's what our president has discovered is the linchpin of higher quality education."

Let's look at that. New Jersey has a teacher/student ratio of 14 students per teacher, ranking second in the nation. Guess which jurisdiction has the smallest teacher/student ratio in the nation. If you said, "It's the nation's capital," go to the head of the class. Washington's teacher/student ratio is 13.7.

A low teacher/student ratio hasn't prevented Washington's students from being just about the nation's dumbest. Japan, whose students run circles around ours, has teacher/student ratios almost double ours.

You say: "But Williams, you're forgetting something else: teacher salaries. The more we pay teachers, the higher the quality of education." Let's look at that.

New Jersey's average teacher salary is $51,000, the nation's fifth-highest. Washington teachers earn $41,000, making them the 16th-highest paid teachers. On the other hand, Minnesota teachers get $38,000, ranked 22nd, and poor Iowa teachers only get $34,000, ranking 34th. With an average salary of $54,000, Massachusetts teacher salaries rank No. 1, while its student achievement ranks 14th.

REAL SOLUTIONS

Nothing the education establishment has called for over the years has or will improve American education. More money and more teachers are nothing more than self-serving strategies to enhance the wealth and power of the education establishment. Solutions to our sorry state of education lie in changing the way education is delivered.

Mike Ramirez. Reprinted by permission of Copley News Service.

The increasing number of charter schools is one alternative. There are 1,129 charter schools operating in 26 states and Washington, D.C., and more are in the works. Their typically higher-than-average scores show that student achievement has little to do with expenditures per student, class size and the number of teachers hired. That fact has been amply demonstrated by private black-owned schools that accommodate poor and moderate-income black students.

Schools such as Marva Collins Preparatory Schools in Cincinnati, Chicago, Milwaukee and Kenosha, Wis.; Ivy Leaf School in

Philadelphia; and Marcus Garvey School in Los Angeles can boast that nearly all of their students score at grade level and above, and at a cost less than half that of public schools.

The education establishment fights tooth and nail to keep its monopoly and avoid accountability. We shouldn't allow its agenda to destroy another generation of American children.

| "States and school districts . . . [should] end the practice of promoting students without regard to how much they have learned."

ENDING SOCIAL PROMOTIONS WOULD IMPROVE ACADEMIC ACHIEVEMENT

Bill Clinton

In the following viewpoint, Bill Clinton argues that public schools must end "social promotions"—the practice of allowing students to move to higher grade levels whether or not they have learned required material. Instead, students should be obligated to meet well-defined academic standards at specific grade levels before passing on to the next level. However, Clinton points out, schools should not simply require unprepared students to repeat a year. Schools should provide smaller classes, well-trained teachers, challenging curricula, after-school programs, and summer-school programs to assist those students who need extra help. Clinton is the forty-second president of the United States. This viewpoint was originally a memorandum sent to the secretary of education.

As you read, consider the following questions:

1. According to Clinton, what are the ultimate consequences of social promotions?
2. In the author's opinion, why should schools avoid simply retaining students in the same grade as a way to end social promotions?
3. What have the public schools in Cincinnati done to end social promotions, according to Clinton?

Reprinted from Bill Clinton, "Memorandum on Helping Schools End Social Promotions," *Weekly Compilation of Presidential Documents*, March 2, 1998.

The linchpin of our efforts to strengthen public education has been to raise standards and expectations for all students. As a result of state and local efforts, and with the support of Goals 2000 and other Federal education programs, students in every state in the country are beginning to benefit from higher academic standards and a more challenging curriculum.

If our efforts to promote higher standards are to lead to increased student achievement, the standards must count. Students must be required to meet them, and schools must provide each student with adequate preparation.

SOCIAL PROMOTIONS

At present, too often standards don't count. Students are passed from grade to grade often regardless of whether they have mastered required material and are academically prepared to do the work at the next level. It's called "social promotion." For many students, the ultimate consequence is that they fall further and further behind, and leave school ill equipped for college and without the skills needed for employment. This is unacceptable for students, teachers, employers, and taxpayers.

That is why I have repeatedly challenged states and school districts to end social promotions—to require students to meet rigorous academic standards at key transition points in their schooling career, and to end the practice of promoting students without regard to how much they have learned. As every parent knows, students must earn their promotion through effort and achievement, not simply by accumulating time in school.

This is especially important in the early grades, where students must acquire a firm foundation in reading in order to learn other subjects in later grade levels. Students should not be promoted past the fourth grade if they cannot read independently and well, and should not enter high school without a solid foundation in math. They should get the help they need to meet the standards before moving on.

THE RIGHT RESPONSE TO LOW ACHIEVEMENT

Neither promoting students when they are unprepared nor simply retaining them in the same grade is the right response to low student achievement. Both approaches presume high rates of initial failure are inevitable and acceptable. Ending social promotions by simply holding more students back is the wrong choice. Students who are required to repeat a year are more likely to eventually drop out, and rarely catch up academically with their peers. The right way is to ensure that more students are prepared to meet challenging academic standards in the first place.

Schools must implement those proven practices that will prepare students to meet rigorous standards the first time. Schools must provide smaller classes, especially for the most disadvantaged students. They must be staffed with well-prepared teachers. Schools should use specific grade-by-grade standards and a challenging curriculum aligned with those standards. They must identify those students who need extra help early on, and provide it immediately. There must be after school and summer school programs for students who need them. The entire school staff must be accountable for results, and must work together as a team to achieve them for every child.

David Horsey. Reprinted by special permission of North America Syndicate.

If steps such as these are taken in every school as part of an overall effort to require students to meet academic standards, we would see a dramatic rise in student achievement and a decline in student retention rates. My administration must help states, school districts, and schools take these steps.

A growing number of states and school districts are responding to the challenge of ending social promotion. A study by the American Federation of Teachers shows that seven states now require school districts and schools to use state standards and assessments to determine if students can be promoted at key grades. We must encourage more states to take this step.

Chicago has also ended social promotions, and instituted a program that provides after school programs for students who need extra help and mandatory summer school for students who do not meet promotion standards. In Cincinnati, student promotion is now based on specific standards that define what students must know and be able to do. The standards are designed to prepare students to pass the state's ninth-grade proficiency test. My administration's proposal to establish education opportunity zones in high poverty urban and rural communities will help more local school systems take these and related steps to help students meet challenging standards.

DESIGNING SUCCESSFUL APPROACHES

As more states and localities move to end social promotions, we must help them design and implement approaches that will succeed. Therefore, I am directing you to take the following actions:

1. *Produce and widely disseminate guidelines for educators and policymakers on effective approaches to ending social promotions.* Drawing on the lessons from research and practice, these guidelines should provide educators and policymakers with practical advice on how to design and implement policies that require students to meet academic standards at key transition points before being promoted. The guidelines should help schools:

- implement strategies that will prepare all students to meet the standards on time;
- end the use of remedial strategies that have been shown to be ineffective;
- provide students who do not meet the standards with immediate and effective extra help—such as after school tutoring programs and summer school—so they can be promoted on time;
- implement effective interventions for students who must be retained; and
- make appropriate use of tests and other indicators of academic performance in determining whether students should be promoted.

2. *Help states and school districts use federal education resources to implement effective practices.* The Department of Education should develop a plan to inform states, school districts, and schools how Department of Education programs and resources, such as Title I, Goals 2000, the 21st Century Schools Program, the Comprehensive School Reform Program, and others, can be used to implement the recommendations in the guidelines described above.

Together, these initiatives can help ensure that our students receive a solid foundation in the basic skills of reading and math, and master advanced subject matters as well. They can help improve the quality of teaching and learning in our schools, and ensure that students who need extra help get it without delay. They can help strengthen our public schools by raising standards, raising expectations, and restoring accountability.

"Research has clearly shown that flunking students to improve their academic performance is ineffective and even harmful."

FLUNKING STUDENTS DOES NOT IMPROVE ACADEMIC ACHIEVEMENT

Ernest R. House

In an effort to improve student performance, some educators advocate retaining low-achieving students at certain grade levels until they have mastered the skills needed to move up to the next level. In the following viewpoint, Ernest R. House maintains that flunking and retaining students does not improve their academic performance and can even be harmful. Studies reveal that students who have been retained are more likely to drop out of school than are similar students who are regularly passed. More effective ways to boost academic achievement include identifying potential problems early on and intervening when poorly performing students are very young, House contends. House is a professor of education at the University of Colorado in Boulder.

As you read, consider the following questions:

1. How many elementary students were held back in Chicago public schools in 1997 and 1998, according to House?
2. What is the annual cost of Chicago's student retention program, according to the author?
3. What is the strategy of "reading recovery," according to House?

Reprinted from Ernest R. House, "Flunking Students Is No Cure-All," *The New York Times*, January 30, 1999, by permission. Copyright ©1999 by The New York Times.

P resident Bill Clinton's latest education proposals have been getting him enthusiastic applause. But on one point, at least, we should be wary.

In his 1999 State of the Union address, Mr. Clinton objected strongly to social promotion—passing students to the next grade level even when they haven't learned very much—and he lauded the "retention" program now being used in Chicago as proof that flunking students improves achievement.

RETENTION IS INEFFECTIVE

One problem with the President's pitch is that no comprehensive evaluation has been conducted of the Chicago program. More broadly, the danger is that advocates of retention will hear only part of the President's words—they will ignore his warning that simply holding students back a grade isn't enough. This would be unfortunate, because research has clearly shown that flunking students to improve their academic performance is ineffective and even harmful.

In fact, school districts in many parts of the country already flunk huge numbers of students. The Chicago system held back about 12,000 elementary students in grades three, six and eight in 1997 and 1998. And New York City is considering going back to a more active use of retention.

All of those involved should learn from the past. In the early 1980's New York City went through one off its periodic cycles of flunking students who weren't keeping up. In a study for the Mayor's office at the time, other educators and I found that the effort was a failure.

Back then, if public school students in grades four and seven did not make a minimum score on a standardized test that year, they were sent to summer school. If they did not achieve the test's cutoff score after summer school, they were held back in special classes. About 25 percent of all fourth and seventh graders were held back in the first year.

These students did not merely repeat the curriculum they had previously failed to master. The city hired 1,100 more teachers so students could be educated in separate, smaller classes of 18. And it gave the teachers of these classes special training.

Nevertheless, after a few years the retained students had gained no more academically than low-achieving students in previous years who had been passed. Later studies showed that the dropout rate for the New York students who flunked was much higher than the rate for similar students who had not been retained.

Numerous studies on retention across the country have yielded similar results. If the evidence is so overwhelming, why does support for retention resurface with such virulence? Because the idea is intuitive, in a way—you have to walk before you can run. But this linear notion of intellectual development ignores some thorny questions. For example, boys and girls develop at different rates, and many more boys are retained.

BETTER SOLUTIONS

Advocates of retention are certainly correct in concluding that it is irresponsible to let students simply drift through ineffective schools. But retention, besides not working, is an awfully costly way to attack that problem. The Chicago effort is costing more than $100 million a year.

There are better ways to spend that kind of money, proven steps that can bolster achievement. The President mentioned a few, like providing extra help to those in need through summer schools and after-school programs, though New York's experience in the 1980's suggests such intervention comes too late for many. A more effective strategy has been "reading recovery." Students who read poorly are identified in first grade. Then specially trained teachers tutor these students on reading skills for one-half hour a day for 12 to 20 weeks. Within a few months these students show remarkable gains in achievement.

THE IMPORTANCE OF EARLY INTERVENTION

Until we recognize where the problem is—long before age six—we will continue to see school failures. The problem is not just schools, but school readiness. To be ready for school, the children have to be healthy. They need appropriate language skills. They must be ready for the social experience of school. They must know how to cooperate with other children, be respectful of the teacher, and understand the importance of doing well in school. To ensure that more children arrive at school ready to learn, we need to invest more in the health, early stimulation, and nurturing of every child born at high risk of failure.

Irving B. Harris, *American Prospect*, September/October 1996.

When a drug is proved unsafe and ineffective, doctors do not continue prescribing it. The failure of widespread retention has been consistently documented. It is nothing more than a way to write off tens of thousands of youngsters.

PERIODICAL BIBLIOGRAPHY

The following articles have been selected to supplement the diverse views presented in this chapter. Addresses are provided for periodicals not indexed in the *Readers' Guide to Periodical Literature*, the *Alternative Press Index*, the *Social Sciences Index*, or the *Index to Legal Periodicals and Books*.

David C. Berliner and Bruce J. Biddle	"Reality-Based Education Standards for All," *Education Digest*, November 1996.
Thomas J. Billitteri	"Teacher Education," *CQ Researcher*, October 17, 1997. Available from Congressional Quarterly, Inc., 1414 22nd St. NW, Washington, DC 20037.
Michael Casserly	"Urban Public Schools on the Comeback," *Education Digest*, February 1999.
Christopher T. Cross and Myron Lieberman	"Symposium: Do Public Schools Need State-Mandated Educational Standards?" *Insight*, February 17, 1997. Available from 3600 New York Ave. NE, Washington, DC 20002.
Jay Gillen	"A Multiple-Choice Problem," *Washington Post National Weekly Edition*, November 17, 1997. Available from 1150 15th St. NW, Washington, DC 20071.
Stephen Goode	"Standard-Bearer," *Insight*, March 1, 1999.
Irving B. Harris	"Starting Small, Thinking Big," *American Prospect*, September/October 1996.
Issues and Controversies On File	"Education Standards," June 27, 1997. Available from Facts On File News Services, 11 Penn Plaza, New York, NY 10001-2006.
Richard C. Kunkel, ed.	Issue on excellence in education, *National Forum*, Winter 1997. Available from the Honor Society of Phi Kappa Phi, Box 16000, Louisiana State University, Baton Rouge, LA 70893.
Diane Ravitch	"Clinton's School Plan Is a Good Start. Let's Go Further," *Wall Street Journal*, January 20, 1999.
James C. Ward	"Why Is School Finance Equity Such an Elusive Goal?" *Rethinking Schools*, Spring 1996.

FOR FURTHER DISCUSSION

CHAPTER 1

1. Karl Zinsmeister contends that the quality of American public education has declined since the mid-1960s. David C. Berliner disagrees, arguing that the overall quality of public education has actually improved since the 1970s. What evidence does each author present to support his conclusion? Whose argument is more persuasive? Why?

2. The authors in this chapter present several arguments describing the causes of what many consider to be a crisis in America's public schools. Compare the various viewpoints, then formulate your own appraisal of the state of public education.

CHAPTER 2

1. Donald Lambro contends that the government should offer tuition vouchers to families so that children can attend the private school of their parents' choice. The National Education Association (NEA) maintains that vouchers will damage public education by taking away needed funds from public schools, thereby increasing educational inequality. Does the NEA's viewpoint effectively refute Donald Lambro's argument? Why or why not?

2. Charles J. Chaput, Reggie White, and Sara White argue that parents should have the right to use vouchers to send their children to Catholic or other religious schools. Llewellyn H. Rockwell argues that voucher programs will harm these schools. How do the arguments of these authors reflect differing views on the nature and purpose of religious schools? Explain your answer, using evidence from the viewpoints.

3. Jeff Jacoby presents the story of the proposed North Bridge Classical Charter School—using quotes from interviews with some of its founding parents—to support his argument for charter schools. Gary Orfield offers several examples of failed and mismanaged charter schools to buttress his argument against them. Which author's technique do you find more compelling? Why?

4. Lawrence W. Reed and Katherine Pfleger have differing opinions on homeschooling as an alternative to public education. According to these authors, what are the potential benefits of homeschooling? What are the potential drawbacks? Do the possible benefits outweigh the drawbacks? Why or why not?

CHAPTER 3

1. James A. Banks contends that one goal of multicultural education is to promote the common good by enabling marginalized groups to participate in the national culture. Thomas J. Famularo disagrees, arguing that multicultural education actually attempts to deny the existence of a distinctive American culture. Which viewpoint do you agree with, and why?

2. Cameron McCarthy decries the lack of minority perspectives in traditional, mainstream history textbooks. Alvin J. Schmidt, however, maintains that multicultural textbooks wrongly malign Euro-American culture and Western civilization. In each viewpoint, try to find two supporting arguments that you personally agree with. Why do you agree with them?

3. Ofelia Garcia and Linda Chavez disagree about the need for public bilingual education programs. How do the arguments of these two authors reflect differing views on the purpose of bilingual education? Whose argument do you find more persuasive?

CHAPTER 4

1. Christina Hoff Sommers maintains that educators should use literature and philosophy to teach uncontroversial ethical values such as integrity, self-control, and sacrifice. How do you think David R. Carlin would respond to Sommers's suggestions? Whose argument do you agree with, and why?

2. Compare the viewpoint of Ann Donnelly with the one written by Tom Peters, Jim Allison, and Susan Batte. For each viewpoint, list the arguments that are based on logical reasoning and those that contain appeals to emotion. In your opinion, which of these authors' arguments is more grounded in logic and which uses more emotional appeals? Defend your answer, using examples from the viewpoints.

3. Robert E. Kofahl contends that creationism should be given "equal time" with evolutionary theory in science curricula. Eugenie Scott argues that creationism has no place in science courses. Kofahl is on the staff of the Creation Science Research Center; Scott is a physical anthropologist who directs the National Center for Science Education. Does knowing their backgrounds influence your assessment of their arguments? Explain your answer.

CHAPTER 5

1. E.D. Hirsch Jr. promotes conservative policies, traditional teaching techniques, and "back-to-basics" learning as ways to improve public education. Deborah Meier advocates community input, personalized instruction, and an emphasis on the development of critical thinking skills as public education reforms. In your opinion, which of these authors' suggestions presents the most effective approach to improving public education? Support your answer with evidence from the viewpoints.

2. The viewpoints in this chapter include several recommendations for improving public education. Consider each recommendation and then list arguments for and against each one. Note whether the arguments are based on facts, values, emotions, or other considerations. If you believe a recommendation should not be considered at all, explain why.

ORGANIZATIONS TO CONTACT

The editors have compiled the following list of organizations concerned with the issues debated in this book. The descriptions are derived from materials provided by the organizations. All have publications or information available for interested readers. The list was compiled on the date of publication of the present volume; the information provided here may change. Be aware that many organizations take several weeks or longer to respond to inquiries, so allow as much time as possible.

Achieve
1280 Massachusetts Ave., Suite 410, Cambridge, MA 02138
(888) 200-0520 • (617) 496-6300 • fax: (617) 496-6361
e-mail: talk-to-us@achieve.org • website: http://www.achieve.org

Achieve's mission is to raise student achievement to world-class levels through the development and implementation of high academic standards, assessments, and accountability systems and the effective use of technology to achieve standards. Its website includes annual reports, information on benchmarking and other initiatives, and a national clearinghouse database for researching academic standards.

American Federation of Teachers (AFT)
555 New Jersey Ave. NW, Washington, DC 20001
(202) 879-4400
e-mail: online@aft.org • website: http://www.aft.org

The American Federation of Teachers is a labor union that represents more than one million teachers, school support staff, higher education faculty and staff, health care professionals, and state and municipal employees. Inside AFT, the union's weekly newsletter, is available at its website.

Association for Supervision and Curriculum Development (ASCD)
1703 N. Beauregard St., Alexandria, VA 22311-1714
(703) 578-9600 • fax: (703) 575-5400
website: http://www.ascd.org

Founded in 1943, the ASCD is an international, nonprofit, nonpartisan education association committed to the mission of forging covenants in teaching and learning to foster the success of all learners. The ASCD provides professional development in curriculum and supervision; initiates and supports activities to promote educational equity for all students; and offers state-of-the-art education information services. The association distributes a variety of journals, newsletters, books, and audio- and videotapes, including The Journal of Curriculum and Supervision, Educational Leadership, and Education Update.

Canadian Education Association (CEA) / Association canadienne d'éducation

252 Bloor St. W., Suite 8-200, Toronto, ON M5S 1V5 CANADA
(416) 924-7721 • fax: (416) 924-3188
e-mail: cea-ace@acea.ca • website: http://www.acea.ca

The CEA is the only national, bilingual, not-for-profit organization promoting public education in Canada. Its publications, which include the *Newsletter/Le Bulletin*, *Education Canada* magazine, and the annual *CEA Handbook*, report on key issues, disseminate educational research, and provide practical information.

Eagle Forum

PO Box 618, Alton, IL 62002
(618) 462-5415 • fax: (618) 462-8909
e-mail: eagle@eagleforum.org • website: http://www.eagleforum.org

The Eagle Forum is an educational and political organization that advocates traditional family values. The forum promotes parental choice of schooling and religious freedom in the classroom and opposes outcome-based education. The organization offers several books and publishes the monthly newsletter *Education Reporter*.

Education Commission of the States (ECS)

707 17th St., #2700, Denver, CO 80202
(303) 299-3600 • fax: (303) 296-8332
e-mail: ecs@ecs.org • website: http://www.ecs.org

The Education Commission of the States is a national nonprofit organization that helps state leaders improve education for all young people. The ECS online service offers information about a host of current issues in education, such as school-to-work policies and programs, various efforts to improve student achievement, school governance, charter schools, and school finance. *State Education Leader* is published three times a year.

FairTest: National Center for Fair & Open Testing

342 Broadway, Cambridge, MA 02139
(617) 864-4810 • fax: (617) 497-2224
e-mail: info@fairtest.org • website: http://www.fairtest.org

FairTest is an advocacy group that opposes the use of standardized tests. It works to end the abuses, misuses, and flaws of standardized testing and to ensure that evaluations are accurate, relevant, and educationally sound. FairTest publishes the quarterly *FairTest Examiner* and offers fact sheets, as well as a catalog of materials, on K–12 and university testing.

The Heritage Foundation

214 Massachusetts Ave. NE, Washington, DC 20002-4999
(202) 546-4400 • fax: (202) 546-8328
e-mail: info@heritage.org • website: http://www.heritage.org

The foundation is a conservative public policy research institute that advocates parental school choice as a means of improving public education. It publishes the quarterly *Policy Review* and other papers and monographs on such issues as political correctness and discrimination in universities.

Home School Legal Defense Association (HSLDA)

PO Box 3000, Purcellville, VA 20134
(540) 338-5600 • fax: (540) 338-2733
e-mail: mailroom@hslda.org • website: http://www.hslda.org

The association is committed to protecting the rights of parents to direct the education of their children. It provides legal assistance to homeschooling families challenged by state government or local school boards. HSLDA publishes *The Home School Court Report* quarterly newsletter and brochures about home education.

The Institute for Creation Research (ICR)

10946 Woodside Ave. N, Santee, CA 92071
(619) 448-0900 • fax: (619) 448-3469
website: http://www.icr.org

The Institute for Creation Research Graduate School is a private not-for-profit corporation which trains students in all scientific disciplines, supplemented with the teachings of scientific creationism. The ICR publishes the monthly news booklet *Acts & Facts* and *Days of Praise*, a quarterly devotional booklet.

National Association of Scholars (NAS)

575 Ewing Street, Princeton, NJ 08540-2741
(609) 683-7878 • fax: (609) 683-0316
e-mail: nas@nas.org • website: http://www.nas.org

The National Association of Scholars is an organization of professors, graduate students, and college administrators committed to academic freedom and the free exchange of ideas in universities. It believes in a curriculum that stresses the achievements of Western civilization and opposes restrictive speech codes, preferences for faculty and students based on race or gender, and an overemphasis on multiculturalism. The NAS publishes the quarterly *Academic Questions.*

National Center for Science Education (NCSE)

PO Box 9477, Berkeley, CA 94709-0477
(800) 290-6006 • (510) 526-1674 • fax: (510) 526-1675
e-mail: ncse@natcenscied.org • website: http://www.natcenscied.org

NCSE is a nonprofit organization working to defend the teaching of evolution against sectarian attack. It is a clearinghouse for information and advice to keep evolution in the science classroom and creationism out. NCSE also works to increase public understanding of evolution and science and has programs to help teachers improve their teaching of evolution. The center publishes books, pamphlets, and the bi-monthly journal, *Reports of NCSE.*

National Council for Black Studies (NCBS)

California State University, Dominguez Hills
1000 East Victoria St., SAC 1115, Carson, CA 90747
(310) 243-2169 • fax: (310) 516-3987
e-mail: ncbs@dhvx20.csudh.edu • website: http://www.eiu.edu/~ncbs/

The NCBS was formed in 1975 out of the substantial need for a national stabilizing force in the developing discipline of Africana/Black Studies. The NCBS believes that education should engender academic excellence and social responsibility, and strongly supports an Afrocentric curriculum for black students. Publications of the council include the *International Journal of Africana Studies* and the newsletter *The Voice of Black Studies*.

National Education Association (NEA)

1201 16th St. NW, Washington, DC 20036
(202) 833-4000
website: http://www.nea.org

The NEA is America's oldest and largest volunteer-based organization dedicated to advancing the cause of public education. Its activities at the local, state, and national levels include conducting professional workshops for teachers, lobbying for needed school resources and higher educational standards, and spearheading innovative projects that reshape the learning process. Two of the NEA's publications, the monthly magazine *NEA Today Online* and biannual report *Thoughts and Action*, are available on its website.

National Parent Teachers Association (PTA)

330 North Wabash Ave., Suite 2100, Chicago, IL 60611-3690
(800) 307-4782 • (312) 670-6782 • fax: (312) 670-6783
e-mail: info@pta.org • website: http://www.pta.org

The PTA is the largest volunteer child advocacy organization in the United States. A not-for-profit organization of parents, educators, students, and other citizens active in their schools and communities, the PTA works to focus national attention on the education, health, and welfare of children. It publishes the magazine *Our Children* and the newsletter *What's Happening in Washington*.

Poverty and Race Research Action Council (PRRAC)

1711 Connecticut Ave. NW, Suite 207, Washington, DC 20009
(202) 387-9887 • fax: (202) 387-0764
e-mail: info@prrac.org • website: http://www.prrac.org

The Poverty and Race Research Action Council is a nonpartisan, national, not-for-profit organization convened by major civil rights, civil liberties, and anti-poverty groups. PRRAC's purpose is to link social science research to advocacy work in order to successfully address problems at the intersection of race and poverty. Its bimonthly publication, *Poverty and Race*, often includes articles on race- and income-based educational inequities in the United States.

U.S. Department of Education
Office of Bilingual Education and Minority Language Affairs
(OBEMLA)
600 Independence Ave. SW, Washington, DC 20202-6510
e-mail: obemla@ed.gov • website: http://www.ed.gov/offices/OBEMLA

The office helps school districts meet their responsibility to provide equal education opportunities to children who are not proficient in English. It provides fact sheets, policy statements, and reports on bilingual education.

BIBLIOGRAPHY OF BOOKS

American Association of University Women, ed. — *Gender Gaps: Where Schools Still Fail Our Children.* New York: Marlowe, 1998.

James A. Banks — *An Introduction to Multicultural Education.* Boston: Allyn and Bacon, 1999.

James A. Banks — *Multiethnic Education: Theory and Practice.* Boston: Allyn and Bacon, 1994.

David C. Berliner and Bruce J. Biddle — *The Manufactured Crisis: Myths, Frauds, and the Attack on America's Public Schools.* Reading, MA: Perseus, 1996.

Heather Bodell — *Goals 2000: A National Framework for America's Schools.* Arlington, VA: Education Funding Research Council, 1994.

Alan Booth and Judith F. Dunn, eds. — *Family-School Links: How Do They Affect Educational Outcomes?* Mahwah, NJ: Lawrence Erlbaum, 1996.

William G. Bowen and Derek Curtis Bok — *The Shape of the River: Long-Term Consequences of Considering Race in College and University Admissions.* Princeton, NJ: Princeton University Press, 1998.

Gerald W. Bracey — *Setting the Record Straight: Responses to Misconceptions About Public Education in the United States.* Alexandria, VA: Association for Supervision and Curriculum Development, 1997.

Vicki A. Brady — *The Basic Steps to Successful Homeschooling.* Lafayette, LA: Vital Issues, 1996.

Maria Estela Brisk — *Bilingual Education: From Compensatory to Quality Education.* Mahwah, NJ: Lawrence Erlbaum, 1997.

Josiah Bunting — *An Education for Our Time.* Washington, DC: Regnery, 1998.

Susan Card and Michael Card — *The Homeschool Journey.* Eugene, OR: Harvest House, 1997.

William Casement — *The Great Canon Controversy: The Battle of the Books in Higher Education.* New Brunswick, NJ: Transaction, 1996.

Mary Beth Celio and Paul Thomas Hill — *Fixing Urban Schools.* Washington, DC: Brookings, 1998.

Robert Coles — *The Moral Intelligence of Children.* New York: Random House, 1997.

William Damon — *The Youth Charter: How Communities Can Work Together to Raise Standards for All Our Children.* New York: Free Press, 1997.

Antinia Darder, Rodolfo D. Torres, and Henry Gutierrez, eds.	*Latinos and Education: A Critical Reader*. New York: Routledge, 1997.
Linda Darling-Hammond	*The Right to Learn: A Blueprint for Creating Schools That Work*. San Francisco: Jossey-Bass, 1997.
Edd Doerr, Albert J. Menendez, and John M. Swomley	*The Case Against School Vouchers*. Amherst, NY: Prometheus Books, 1996.
John M. Ellis	*Literature Lost: Social Agendas and the Corruption of the Humanities*. New Haven, CT: Yale University Press, 1997.
Williamson M. Evers	*What's Gone Wrong in America's Classrooms*. Stanford, CA: Hoover Institution, 1998.
Paulo Freire	*Pedagogy of the Oppressed*. New York: Continuum, 1995.
Bruce Fuller, Richard F. Elmore, and Gary Orfield, eds.	*Who Chooses? Who Loses?: Culture, Institutions, and the Unequal Effects of School Choice*. New York: Teachers College Press, 1996.
Roberta Furger	*Does Jane Compute?: Preserving Our Daughters' Place in the Cyber Revolution*. New York: Warner Books, 1998.
Barbara B. Gaddy	*School Wars: Resolving Our Conflicts over Religion and Values*. San Francisco: Jossey-Bass, 1996.
Henry A. Giroux	*Living Dangerously: Multiculturalism and the Politics of Difference*. New York: P. Lang, 1993.
Bruce Goldberg	*Why Schools Fail*. Washington, DC: Cato, 1996.
Kenneth S. Goodman, ed.	*In Defense of Good Teaching: What Teachers Need to Know About the "Reading Wars."* York, ME: Stenhouse, 1998.
Sunny Hansen, Joyce Walker, and Barbara Flom	*Growing Smart: What's Working for Girls in School*. Washington, DC: American Association of University Women Educational Foundation, 1995.
E.D. Hirsch	*The Schools We Need and Why We Don't Have Them*. New York: Doubleday, 1996.
Freeman A. Hrabowski, Kenneth I. Maton, and Geoffrey L. Greif	*Beating the Odds: Raising Academically Successful African American Males*. New York: Oxford University Press, 1998.
Thomas C. Hunt and James C. Carper, eds.	*Religion and Schooling in Contemporary America: Confronting Our Cultural Pluralism*. New York: Garland, 1997.
Jacqueline Jordan Irvine and Michele Foster, eds.	*Growing Up African American in Catholic Schools*. New York: Teachers College Press, 1996.
John F. Jennings	*Why National Standards and Tests?: Politics and the Quest for Better Schools*. Thousand Oaks, CA: Sage, 1998.

Joseph Kahne — *Reframing Educational Policy: Democracy, Community, and the Individual.* New York: Teachers College Press, 1996.

Roger Kimball — *Tenured Radicals: How Politics Has Corrupted Our Higher Education.* Chicago: Elephant Paperbacks, 1998.

Edward J. Larson — *Summer for the Gods: The Scopes Trial and America's Continuing Debate over Science and Religion.* New York: Basic-Books, 1997.

Jay Mathews — *Class Struggle: What's Wrong (and Right) with America's Best Public High Schools.* New York: Times Books, 1998.

Maralee Mayberry et al. — *Home Schooling: Parents as Educators.* Thousand Oaks, CA: Corwin, 1995.

Elaine K. McEwan — *Angry Parents, Failing Schools: What's Wrong with the Public Schools and What You Can Do About It.* Wheaton, IL: Harold Shaw, 1998.

Daniel McGroarty and William J. Bennett — *Break These Chains: The Battle for School Choice.* Rocklin, CA: Prima, 1996.

Deborah Meier — *The Power of Their Ideas: Lessons for America from a Small School in Harlem.* Boston: Beacon, 1996.

Richard E. Miller — *As If Learning Mattered: Reforming Higher Education.* Ithaca, NY: Cornell University Press, 1998.

Alex Molnar — *The Construction of Children's Character.* Chicago: University of Chicago Press, 1997.

Joe Nathan — *Charter Schools: Creating Hope and Opportunity for American Education.* San Francisco: Jossey-Bass, 1996.

Sonia Nieto — *Affirming Diversity: The Sociopolitical Context of Multicultural Education.* Reading, MA: Addison-Wesley, 1996.

Warren A. Nord — *Religion and American Education: Rethinking a National Dilemma.* Chapel Hill: University of North Carolina Press, 1995.

Martha Craven Nussbaum — *Cultivating Humanity: A Classical Defense of Reform in Liberal Education.* Cambridge, MA: Harvard University Press, 1998.

Jeannie Oakes and Karen Hunter Quartz, eds. — *Creating New Educational Communities.* Chicago: University of Chicago Press, 1995.

Paul E. Peterson and Bryan C. Hassel, eds. — *Learning from School Choice.* Washington, DC: Brookings, 1998.

Delvin Lee Ratzsch — *The Battle of Beginnings: Why Neither Side Is Winning the Creation-Evolution Debate.* Downers Grove, IL: InterVarsity, 1996.

Diane Ravitch	*National Standards in Education: A Citizen's Guide.* Washington, DC: Brookings, 1995.
Diane Ravitch and Maris A. Vinovskis, eds.	*Learning from the Past: What History Teaches Us About School Reform.* Baltimore: Johns Hopkins University Press, 1995.
Laura I. Rendon et al.	*Educating a New Majority: Transforming America's Educational System for Diversity.* San Francisco: Jossey-Bass, 1996.
Richard Rothstein	*The Way We Were?: The Myths and Realities of America's Student Achievement.* New York: Century Foundation, 1998.
Seymour Bernard Sarason	*Charter Schools: Another Flawed Educational Reform?* New York: Teachers College Press, 1998.
Alvin J. Schmidt	*The Menace of Multiculturalism: Trojan Horse in America.* Westport, CT: Praeger, 1997.
James T. Sears and James C. Carper, eds.	*Curriculum, Religion, and Public Education: Conversations for an Enlarging Public Square.* New York: Teachers College Press, 1998.
Joel H. Spring	*Political Agendas for Education: From the Christian Coalition to the Green Party.* Mahwah, NJ: Lawrence Erlbaum, 1997.
Laurence Steinberg et al.	*Beyond the Classroom: Why School Reform Has Failed and What Parents Need to Do.* New York: Touchstone Books, 1997.
Charles J. Sykes	*Dumbing Down Our Kids: Why American Children Feel Good About Themselves but Can't Read, Write, or Add.* New York: St. Martin's, 1996.
Marc S. Tucker and Judy B. Codding	*Standards for Our Schools: How to Set Them, Measure Them, and Reach Them.* New York: Simon & Schuster, 1998.
Diana Waring and Cathy Duffy	*Beyond Survival: A Guide to Abundant-Life Homeschooling.* Lynnwood, WA: Emerald Books, 1996.
Ronald A. Welk et al., eds.	*Quality Counts: A Report Card on the Condition of Public Education in the 50 States.* Washington, DC: Editorial Projects in Education, 1997.
John K. Wilson	*The Myth of Political Correctness: The Conservative Attack on Higher Education.* Durham, NC: Duke University Press, 1995.

INDEX

abortion, 142, 147
academic achievement, 12, 26
  decline in, 17, 19, 20, 21
    declared by every generation, 27
    due to inequities between school
      districts, 41, 42, 43
      that can be overcome, 44–45
    due to progressive theories of
      education, 174–77
    due to superficial learning and
      curricula, 22, 23–24
    and early intervention, 202
    funding not related to, 192–93
    and ineffectiveness of student
      retention, 200–201
    less time in school a factor in, 30
    low expectations a cause of, 37–40
    and need to clarify goals, 24–25
    and need to end social promotion
      of failing students, 196–98, 199
  lack of commitment to, 32–34
  ways to improve, 29, 34–36, 195
  see also Scholastic Assessment Test
    (SAT); teacher training
Adams, Jane, 113
adolescent peer groups, 34
affirmative action, 127, 147
Africa and Africans (Thornton), 120–21
African Americans, 12, 67, 73, 83, 111
  and black-owned private schools,
    193–94
  and college admissions, 127
  Denver public school system sued by,
    65
  lower success rate among, 43, 176
    not linked to capability, 44
  and multicultural education, 100,
    101, 102
  and school segregation, 188–89
Afro-Asian Black Arts movement
  (England), 110
after-school employment, 35–36
Alexis de Tocqueville Institution, 68
Ali, Muhammad, 101
Allen, John, 44
Allen, Joy, 68, 69
Allison, Jim, 152
America: Past and Present (Anderson &
  King), 114, 115
American Civil Liberties Union
  (ACLU), 55, 146
American Educator (journal), 111

American Enterprise, 18
American Enterprise Institute, 137, 138
American Federation of Teachers, 197
American Indians. See Native Americans
American Odyssey (Nash), 124
American Prospect, 29, 202
American Scholar, The (journal), 104, 112
Analects (Confucius), 143
Anderson, C., 114
Angelou, Maya, 101
antitraditional schools, 18
  parents unaware about, 19
  see also charter schools;
    homeschooling; progressive
    education
Arizona, 78, 81
Asia, 31, 98
Asian Americans, 31, 73, 102
Attucks, Crispus, 119, 123
Au, Kathryn, 99

Ball State University, 75
Baltimore, 91
Banks, James A., 95, 96, 100
Bass, Lee M., 104
Batte, Susan, 152
Bell, Terrel H., 169
Bennett, William, 27, 31, 145
Berliner, David C., 13, 16, 26
Bernstein, Richard, 104
Bertonneau, Thomas, 47, 49
Bible, 143, 147, 156, 160
Biddle, Bruce J., 13
bilingual education, 126
  benefits of, 128–29
  failure of, 130–34
  inclusiveness of, 127
Black History Month, 116
Black Jacobins, The (James), 115
Bloom, Allan, 111
Boston Massacre, 119, 123
Boston University, 132
Bowen, Roger W., 82
Bracey, Gerald W., 29
Breyer, Stephen, 55
Brown, Cheryl, 69
Brown v. Board of Education, 19, 106, 188
Bush, George, 81
Byrne, David, 110

California, 23, 140–41, 158, 174
  ban on affirmative action in, 127